Walking

Shannon Manley Bales

Copyright © 2025

All Rights Reserved

ISBN: 979-8-90056-807-2

Published by: WALKING PROOF LLC, Portage, Indiana

© 2025 Shannon Manley Bales

walkingproof@myyahoo.com

www.WalkingProof.net

Printed in the United States of America

Dedication

To Sybil Ray Tennyson Stevens, my birth mother, who endured a life full of physical and sexual assaults, mental illness, and homelessness.

You live with more pain than most can see, battling the weight of mental illness in a world that rarely makes space for your healing.

You did not raise me, but your decision to leave was an act of survival – a choice shaped by trauma, fear, and strength.

This book is about my search for the man who hurt you, the father I never truly knew, and in that search, I began to understand you more clearly: your silences, your distance, your sorrow.

Though our relationship was shaped more by absence than presence, your story lives at the heart of this one.

I carry it with tenderness, complexity, and care.

This is for you – not as a celebration or a reconciliation, but as a recognition of your humanity.

Acknowledgment

First, I want to thank my husband, ***Joseph Carl Bales*** – you spent countless hours encouraging me, researching, editing, and supporting me throughout this project. Your steady love and unwavering support these past sixteen years have carried me through some of the darkest, most confusing parts of this journey. You've held my hand through heartbreak and reminded me who I am when I started to forget. I love you deeply.

To my mother-in-law, ***Carolyn "Callie" Dyess Bales*** – thank you for gifting me that DNA kit. You had no idea what doors it would open or the truth it would reveal. That simple act, the Christmas gift in 2009, unlocked answers to decades of mystery, crime, and genealogy. You've always treated me like your own, and I'm forever grateful.

To my late mom, ***Catherine Ann Kay Roark*** – thank you for raising me with strength, compassion, and faith. You were 58 when you took me in at just two weeks old and raised me as your own. Even though the circumstances of my birth were hidden from us both, your love was never in question. I carry it with me still. I appreciate all your sacrifices; you are missed!

To my ***family and friends*** – thank you for listening when I needed to process, for encouraging me to keep going, and for not shrinking away from the hard parts. Your belief in me gave me the courage to finish. The leads and information you provided made this project possible.

To the *families of the victims* – your pain is unimaginable. I didn't write this book to reopen wounds but to acknowledge the truth, to hold it up to the light, and to make sure your stories are not forgotten.

And finally, to *everyone* reading this who is searching, questioning, or trying to put the pieces of their own story together – you are not alone. Truth has a way of finding us, even when we're not looking.

About the Author

Shannon Manley Bales is a DNA detective, author, and advocate for truth and healing. Born and raised in Houston, Texas, he now lives in Miller Beach, a beachfront community in Gary, Indiana, with his husband Joseph. He spent his career in finance before discovering a new purpose through genetic genealogy.

His own life took a dramatic turn when a DNA test unraveled long-hidden family secrets and led him to uncover his biological father's connection to unsolved crimes. What began as a personal journey evolved into a mission to help others find their roots, reunite families, and shine a light on injustice.

Shannon always knew he had a book buried deep inside of him, just waiting for the right time to develop and come to fruition. Shannon's career in banking and managing collection agencies helped develop the skip-tracing and research skills, which became valuable tools to write *Walking Proof*, his debut book filled with mystery, rape, murder, cold cases, and true crime.

Shannon, a proud stepfather and grandfather to Joseph's two children and five grandchildren, enjoys traveling to the Houston area in the winter – their snowbird destination since retirement. When he's not writing and researching, Shannon can be found hiking, camping, and helping others navigate the emotional and legal complexities of family discovery.

Preface

I never set out to write a book.

Like most people, I took a DNA test just to learn a little more about where I came from. Maybe find a few cousins. Maybe confirm some old family stories. I wasn't prepared for what I found – or what it would demand of me.

What started as a simple curiosity unraveled everything I thought I knew about my identity. I learned that I was the product of rape – something no child should ever have to reckon with, yet something that shaped the very foundation of my life. My biological father was a stranger, one whose past held secrets darker than anything I could've imagined. And suddenly, I found myself in the middle of a story that stretched far beyond my own life – into decades-old cold cases, broken systems, and families still searching for justice.

Walking Proof is about more than just my journey. It's a story about confronting painful truths, even when they blindside you. It's about what it means to carry trauma in your blood – and how healing can still grow from that place. There may be those who are questioning where they came from, those who may still be searching – my hope is that this book will be the inspiration – for those who are brave enough – to follow the truth – no matter how difficult the path.

Contents

Dedication i
Acknowledgment ii
About the Author iv
Preface v
Chapter 1: The Christmas Gift 1
Chapter 2: The Warning Signs 17
Chapter 3: The Brutal Truth 43
Chapter 4: The Hunt Begins 65
Chapter 5: A Darker Pattern Emerges 86
Chapter 6: Deadly Coincidences 109
Chapter 7: Digging into the Past 117
Chapter 8: Built on Circumstance 128
Chapter 9: Confirmation 146
Chapter 10: An Unconventional Relationship 172
Chapter 11: Reasonable Doubts, Relentless Questions 194
Chapter 12: Born of a Storm, Carried by the Tide 217
Chapter 13: Sources and Resources 228

Chapter 1: The Christmas Gift

Christmas 2009 was supposed to be a quiet one. I had been invited to spend the holiday with the family of the man I had started dating, a relatively new relationship that felt promising yet uncertain. Being the newcomer among them, I kept to the background, smiling politely, making small talk when necessary, and watching as presents were passed around the living room. The warmth of the holiday filled the space – laughter, the clinking of glasses, the occasional gasp of delight when a particularly thoughtful gift was revealed. It had been a long time since I felt included in something like this.

Then, someone handed me a small box. I looked up to see his mother smiling at me expectantly.

"Go on, open it," she encouraged, her eyes warm with something between affection and curiosity.

I peeled away the wrapping paper and lifted the lid. A DNA testing kit. A simple, ordinary box that so many people had opened before me without a second thought. But for me, it was something else entirely. It was an invitation to answers I had never sought, a question I hadn't even asked out loud. At that moment, it was just a gift, nothing more. But I couldn't have known then how much this tiny box would change everything.

I never imagined this gift, innocent in appearance, wrapped in cheerful paper, would be the beginning of something far more sinister. I didn't realize that inside was the first clue – a thread that, once pulled, would unravel everything I thought I knew about myself. Before it was over, it would uncover a trail of violent crime… and reveal that my bloodline carried even darker secrets.

Before I opened the Christmas gift, I quickly reflected on my life's history. The gravity of the many things I had been through by that time, and the weight of those experiences, shaped how I felt at that moment. The thoughts going through my head and the emotions overwhelming my heart helped me process the reaction I was feeling when I received this gift.

I had spent my life surrounded by losses. By the time I was three, I had already lost my biological mother and the only father I had ever known. Early on, I learned that love wasn't always permanent, that family could be fleeting, and that sometimes the people who were supposed to be there forever simply weren't.

My biological mother, Sybil Ray Tennyson – affectionately known to me as Mother Sybil – had given birth to me, but wasn't the one who raised me. She left me with my great-uncle and great-aunt when I was just two weeks old, dropping me off at their home with what I assume were the best of intentions.

Maybe she thought she would come back for me when she was ready. Maybe she believed I would be better off with them. Or maybe she simply didn't know what else to do. Whatever her reasons, she never returned, and my life took its first major detour before I was old enough to understand what that meant.

My great-uncle and great-aunt, Sherrill and Catherine Roark, were not young when they took me in. They were at an age when they should have been enjoying the lives of grandparents, not raising an infant.

Sherrill was 68, Catherine 58. They had never had children of their own, but now, suddenly, they were parents. They never made me feel unwanted, though. In fact, they embraced the role, becoming Uncle Daddy and Auntie Momma to me. They were my entire world.

Then, in January of 1983, that world shifted again. Catherine, Auntie Momma had fallen ill with pneumonia and was hospitalized. Sherrill, Uncle Daddy spent his days visiting her, ensuring she was cared for, and keeping the house running in her absence. And then, one night, as he was driving home from the hospital, tragedy struck.

A Houston Power and Light company truck, driven by an on-duty employee, crashed into him. The injuries were catastrophic. Uncle Daddy survived the initial accident, but the damage was too severe. He fought for two months, but on March 28, 1983, he took his last breath. I was three years old. Too young to understand but not too young to feel the loss. He was the only father I had ever known, and suddenly, he was gone.

Auntie Momma became a single parent overnight. At an age when most people were preparing for retirement, she was raising a toddler alone. I don't know how she did it. I don't think I ever truly gave her enough credit for how much she took on when she chose to be my mother in every way that mattered.

When I reached school age, things shifted again. The world started calling Catherine my mom, and I followed suit. It was a natural transition that reflected our relationship's truth. The woman who had given birth to me simply became Sybil in my mind.

Church became everything. It was my community, my stability. Catherine, mom had her own struggles – mental health issues that made life unpredictable at times – but the church filled in the gaps. It gave me a sense of belonging, of purpose. I grew up knowing the rhythms of Sunday mornings, the exuberant worship of the Sunday evening choir, and the weight of expectation from being raised in a congregation that saw me as one of their own.

In 1993, my mom was diagnosed with pulmonary fibrosis, and life took another shift. She was only given a couple of years to live, so she took me out of school and applied for a hardship driver's license so I could transport her to and from her doctor's appointments. I then found myself at fourteen years old as the primary caregiver for my seventy-two-year-old mom. On January 6, 2000, seven years later, my mom finally succumbed to her illness and passed away.

At nineteen, I thought I had found my forever family. I married a woman from my church background, believing we would build the life I had always imagined together. Stability. Love. A home filled with warmth and belonging. It was supposed to be my happy-ever-after family.

Instead, it was another loss.

By January 2006, our marriage of six and a half years had unraveled and ended in divorce. I was left standing in the wreckage of a life I had tried so hard to build, realizing that maybe I had never truly belonged there.

Then came another truth I could no longer ignore. My sexual orientation. It wasn't something I had just discovered – it had been there all along, quietly pressing against the edges of my carefully constructed life. But now, without the constraints of marriage holding me in place, I had to face it. I came out. And with that, I lost something else.

The church that had been my home, foundation, and family suddenly felt like enemy territory. Based on my preconceived ideas from the teachings and sermons I had heard my entire life, I believed they would turn their backs on me, seeing me as something broken, something lost. It was a loss that cut deeper than I had expected. I had spent my entire life looking for a place where I belonged, and now it felt like I had lost my last chance at finding it.

I entered into a relationship with a man. It was a year filled with highs and lows, passion and conflict, hope and heartbreak. When it ended, I was left alone again, wondering if real, lasting love was something I would ever truly find.

So, when I sat there on Christmas Day in 2009, holding that DNA kit in my hands, I wasn't thinking about family. I wasn't thinking about what it meant, what it could reveal. It was just another gift. A novelty. I was happy that I was thought of and sincerely appreciated the effort that his mother had put into giving me a gift.

I didn't know yet that I was holding the key to another truth. Another shift in my world. Another answer to a question I hadn't even known to ask.

For now, though, it was just a box. And I had no idea what was coming next because life had a way of surprising me. However, by 2009, I had long since stopped expecting good surprises. I had lost so much – my biological mother through abandonment, my father, the mom who raised me, my marriage, my church family, my first same-sex relationship, and the sense of security that had held me together for so long. And yet, life kept moving, even when I felt stuck, even when I wasn't sure what I was supposed to hold on to anymore.

In the midst of this loss, in the middle of trying to figure out how to rebuild, I met Joseph Bales.

I wasn't looking for a relationship. I wasn't looking for much of anything. I had just wanted to find a place where I could feel a little less lost. A church in Houston had seemed like a good start – familiar ground, even if my relationship with faith was more complicated than ever. The church had been my foundation once. Maybe it could be again.

Joseph was one of the first people I met there. He was warm in a way that caught me off guard, easy to talk to, with a quiet steadiness that made me feel, for the first time in a long time, like I wasn't just drifting. He was from Louisiana, born and raised in a small town that was totally opposite the metropolitan area of Houston, where I had grown up. His upbringing had been shaped by the same kind of strict, conservative United Pentecostal Church environment that had defined so much of my early years.

Maybe that was part of what drew me to him – our similar religious backgrounds, his deep love for family, and the empathy and compassion he showed toward others, especially those less fortunate.

We started spending more time together, first as friends. Then, in September 2009, something shifted, and we began dating.

I was hesitant. I had been hurt before. I had spent years believing I knew what love was supposed to look like, only to have that belief shattered. And yet, there was something about Joseph that felt safe. Like maybe, just maybe, I could find family again.

That was how I began meeting his family in the fall of 2009.

Joseph's family was nothing like mine. They were loud, open, and always in each other's business. There were family dinners with too many people crammed around a table, stories that had been told so many times that everyone already knew the punchlines, and a kind of unconditional love I hadn't realized I had been missing.

I was cautious at first, unsure of my place. But they welcomed me in as if I had always belonged.

And then, in December, Joseph's mother gave me the Christmas gift that changed everything.

The DNA test had been meant as a fun gesture, a way to learn more about my ancestry, to connect me to the past in a way that, at the time, I thought would be simple. I didn't know that I would be unraveling a history I hadn't even known was tangled in opening that box.

My story didn't begin with me. It didn't even begin with my mother. It was a story that stretched back generations, with choices and secrets that had shaped the very foundation of my life.

I had always known that my birth mother, Sybil, had a complicated past.

Sybil married Jimmy Stockstill in January 1978. From what I had gathered over the years, their marriage had been rocky from the start – on again, off again, full of arguments and separations.

By the time I was born on July 25, 1979, they were no longer together. My mother hadn't even taken Jimmy's last name, so I was named Shannon Lee Manley.

Jimmy Stockstill had a life before my mother. He had been married once before and had two sons from that marriage. That marriage, too, had ended badly – apparently, when it was discovered that while he was imprisoned in Mexico, he had fathered a child. That child, my half-sister, Yessica Guzman, was born exactly two years before me on July 25, 1977.

Details of Yessica's conception are varied. How Jimmy managed to obtain conjugal visits is a mystery. Nonetheless, while in jail, Jimmy fathered a daughter, Yessica, with a fourteen-year-old girl.

That was the family I had never known. That was the bloodline I hadn't realized I was connected to.

Jimmy had never been in my life. He and Sybil had barely stayed together long enough for me to exist. I had grown up with limited knowledge of him, raised by Catherine, the woman who had stepped into the role of mother when Sybil had abandoned me. Catherine, mom, was there when I needed her the most.

I had spent so many years thinking that the losses I had experienced were just a part of life. My family had been small because of the hand I had been dealt. I had been alone in so many ways because that was how it was always meant to be.

Every Christmas from the age of twelve until my first marriage, I spent alone. My mom would give me a one-hundred-dollar bill and drop me off at the mall to watch a movie while she visited with her sisters and their families.

However, that DNA test, that simple Christmas gift, was about to prove me wrong.

Joseph's mother, Carolyn – Callie, as everyone called her – had a way of making people feel at home. She was one of those women who could light up a room just by walking into it, with her bright red hair, booming laugh, and the kind of presence that made you feel like you mattered. She loved her family. She loved history. And more than anything, she loved weaving those two things together.

Christmas was her season.

I had only met Callie twice – once over Halloween and again at Thanksgiving at Joseph's house in Beaumont, Texas. Both times, she'd been warm and welcoming, the kind of person who could size you up instantly and still find something to like about you. But I wasn't family. Not yet. And when it came time for Christmas gifts, she had no idea what to get me.

So, she did what any logical person would do – she called Joseph.

"What does Shannon like?" she asked. "What would be meaningful to him?"

Joseph, bless him, didn't have an easy answer. I wasn't the kind of person who collected things. I didn't have hobbies that could be neatly packaged and put under a tree. My life, for the most part, had been about survival.

He did mention my past. My lack of a real connection to my biological family. I knew next to nothing about the people who had come before me.

That was all Callie needed to hear.

A few days later, she ordered a Family Tree DNA kit and wrapped it up with a bow. Christmas with Joseph's family was going to be an event. I knew that before we even got in the car.

His family did things big. Big gatherings, big meals, big personalities. They weren't just celebrating the holiday – they were celebrating each other. Every year, dozens of relatives piled into a single house, cramming into every available seat, filling the air with conversation and laughter.

I was about to step into the middle of it.

The drive to Alexandria, Louisiana, was a quiet one. I was nervous. Not because I thought they'd be unkind – Joseph had repeatedly assured me that his family was warm and accepting. But there was something about walking into a house full of people with decades of shared history, who knew each other inside and out, who belonged in a way I never had.

What if I didn't fit?

What if I were just another outsider passing through?

I sat in the passenger seat, watching the road signs blur past, my hands twisting in my lap. Joseph reached over and gave my knee a squeeze.

"They're going to love you," he said. "Callie already does."

I forced a smile. I wanted to believe him. It was like a house that felt like a town. When we pulled into the driveway, the house looked bigger than I'd imagined. Or maybe it was just that the sheer number of cars made it feel that way. Every inch of pavement was filled, SUVs and sedans packed in like puzzle pieces, kids running between them, squealing with an excitement that only Christmas could bring.

Inside, it was chaos – but the best kind. The smell of roasted ham and candied yams filled the air, mingling with the crisp scent of pine from the Christmas tree in the corner. Every room was packed with people. Aunts, uncles, cousins, kids, friends who might as well have been family.

And in the middle of it all was Callie.

She spotted us from across the room and walked over, weaving through the crowd like she'd been born for it.

"Shannon!" she said, pulling me into a hug before I even had time to react. I tensed at first. Hugs weren't something I was used to, not from people who barely knew me. But she held on, firm and warm like she was grounding me in place.

"It's so good to see you," she said, stepping back to get a good look at me. "Are you ready for some real Christmas spirit?"

I nodded, managing a small smile.

"Good," she said. "Come on, let's get you fed."

Dinner was loud and long and full of laughter. Plates were passed back and forth, stories were told, and I felt a little less like an outsider by the time we were done.

Then came the gifts.

Callie had a present for everyone: a small token of love wrapped up in paper and ribbons. When she handed me my box, she looked excited, like she knew something I didn't. I peeled back the wrapping paper and lifted the lid.

Inside was a DNA kit.

For a second, I just stared at it. I'd never even considered doing something like this before. It had always seemed pointless. What would I even be looking for? But Callie had thought of it. She had looked at me – this near-stranger, this man who had lost nearly everything – and decided I deserved to know where I came from.

I swallowed hard.

"You don't have to do it," she said quickly, "only if you want to."

I shook my head.

"No, I... I want to."

Suddenly, I did. Callie helped me with the test, walking me through each step. It was simple – just a swab of my cheek, a quick seal, and then sending it off to a lab. Nothing dramatic. Nothing complicated.

But as I held the little test tube in my hand, I realized how much weight it carried. I had never known my biological father's family. Not really. And now, in a few months' time, I would have answers. Callie grinned at me.

"I think you're going to find some interesting things."

I smiled back, but inside, I felt a strange mix of excitement and anxiety.

What if I didn't like what I found? What if I did?

Callie had been right – this DNA test was the perfect gift. But now that the results were sitting in front of me, I wasn't sure if I was ready for them. Joseph leaned in, waiting for me to click the link. His arm was warm against mine, steady in a way I desperately needed.

I exhaled and clicked. The page loaded, and my heart thudded in my chest as I scanned the names. At first, nothing registered. It was a jumble of distant relatives, percentages, and unfamiliar surnames. I scrolled, searching for something – anything – that made sense.

And then, confusion set in.

There were no Stockstills. Not one.

I checked again, and I was sure I had missed something. But the same names kept appearing: Williams. Dixon. More Williamses. More Dixons. My stomach tightened as I turned to Joseph.

"I don't see any Stockstills."

He frowned, leaning in closer.

"Are you sure? Check the paternal matches."

I did. Again. Nothing. A cold wave of uncertainty washed over me.

"What does this mean?" I asked.

Joseph didn't answer right away. He was staring at the screen, thinking.

"Maybe…" he hesitated, "maybe there's a mistake?"

But we both knew DNA tests didn't make mistakes – not like this.

I stared at the names, willing them to change, willing a Stockstill to appear. But all I saw were Williamses and Dixons. My mind started racing.

Maybe Jimmy had been adopted, and no one knew. Maybe the Stockstill name had been a cover for something else? That would mean Jimmy could still possibly be my father.

A lump formed in my throat.

Maybe the man I thought was my father wasn't my father at all, but maybe he was.

I swallowed hard, "I don't understand."

Joseph placed a hand on my shoulder, "We'll figure it out."

But neither of us had any idea what that would mean.

The next few days were a blur of research, phone calls, and dead ends. I spent hours combing through my DNA results, clicking on every match, scanning through distant relatives' profiles, and trying to piece something together. Every name I reached out to had one thing in common: none of them had ever heard of the Manley or Stockstill families.

I sat in my office, laptop open, frustration building with every unanswered email and every polite, confused response. I had expected answers. Instead, I had more questions than ever.

Who were the Williamses and Dixons? And why weren't there any Stockstills?

Rubbing my temples, I stared at the screen. My DNA was staring back at me, undeniable, unchangeable, and raising questions I never thought I'd have to ask.

If my father wasn't a Stockstill, then who was he? Who was I?

The thought made my chest tighten. I had always believed I knew my roots, even if I hadn't explored them deeply. Now, the foundation of everything I assumed was crumbling.

I took a deep breath and kept searching.

Chapter 2: The Warning Signs

Aunt Anita didn't hesitate. She cut me off when I told her about my DNA test results.

"Stop looking," she said.

It wasn't a suggestion. It wasn't a casual remark. It was a warning.

I pressed the phone closer to my ear, hoping I had misunderstood, "What do you mean?"

"You don't need to look," she repeated, her voice measured but firm. "Sherrill was a great father."

Sherrill – Uncle Daddy. The man who raised me until I was three before a traffic accident took him away. He wasn't my biological father, and I had never thought he was. But that wasn't what I was asking.

"Aunt Anita," I said slowly, carefully, "I'm not questioning that. I just… I need to know where I come from. The DNA results –"

"No," she interrupted, "you don't."

I sat there, gripping the phone, my pulse drumming in my ears. Aunt Anita wasn't just refusing to help me. She shut the door before I even had a chance to step through it.

"Why?" I asked.

A long pause. I could hear her breathing and the muffled sound of a television in the background.

"You're not going to find what you're looking for, Shannon," she finally said, "and even if you do, you won't like it."

I exhaled, forcing my voice to stay even, "But you know something."

Another pause.

"I'm telling you," she said, "let it be."

The call ended, and I sat there, staring at my phone, Aunt Anita's words looping in my head.

Let it be.

But how could I?

I had accepted the story my family told me for most of my life. My mother, Sybil Ray Tennyson, had been married to Jimmy Stockstill when she got pregnant with me. That was the narrative. Simple. Clean.

But it was never that simple.

There were always whispers – stray comments at family gatherings, things half-heard and never explained. I knew that Sybil and Jimmy's marriage was short and volatile. I knew that people in my family had spoken about "rape" when I was growing up, though no one ever elaborated.

I had always assumed, without pushing too hard, that Jimmy Stockstill was my father and that my conception was the result of some kind of domestic violence during the rocky, on-again, off-again period following their divorce.

Then, as I got older, I learned more. I found Jimmy's name on the sex offender registry. That, more than anything, made the rumors of rape seem plausible. But now, with the DNA results in front of me, that version of the truth was unraveling.

Stockstill wasn't my bloodline.

So, if Jimmy wasn't my father, then who was?

And why didn't Aunt Anita want me to find out?

I started digging deeper into Sybil's past, hoping to make sense of the fragments I had.

Sybil and her twin sister, Anita, were born on June 6, 1953, to Raymond Randolph Tennyson and Myrtle Blossom Morris.

They had a rough start. According to medical records and family accounts, their mother, Myrtle, abandoned them when they were still infants. Their father, Raymond, and his mother, Etta Pearl, raised the girls until their deaths when the twins were just eleven years old.

After that, Sybil and Anita bounced between relatives, shifting from household to household, never truly settling.

Even though they were twins, they were as different as two people could be.

Sybil was the extrovert. Blonde hair, piercing blue eyes, and a social butterfly who could charm anyone she met. She was magnetic, spontaneous, and lived in the moment.

Anita was the opposite. She had striking red hair and a rare, almost ghostly shade of gray-blue eyes. She was introverted, a bookworm who found comfort in knowledge rather than chaos.

Their paths diverged early.

On January 5, 1971, at just seventeen years old, Sybil married Harold Glen Manley. Three years later, on August 1, 1974, she gave birth to a daughter, Christy.

The marriage didn't last.

Sybil and Harold divorced less than six years later, on May 20, 1977.

And then came Jimmy. She met him not long after the divorce, and on February 9, 1978, they got married. It wasn't a love story. Not really. Their marriage lasted four months. The divorce was finalized on June 27, 1978, but that didn't mean he was gone.

Their relationship was toxic, the kind that didn't end cleanly. They broke up, got back together, and broke up again. It was a cycle, one that never fully stopped. And in the middle of that *chaos*, I was conceived.

On July 25, 1979, Sybil gave birth to me.

She named me Shannon Lee Manley.

Not Stockstill.

Even though she married Jimmy, she never legally changed her last name to his.

Even though everyone said he was my father, she hadn't given me his name. Sybil did not even list a father on my birth certificate.

That small detail had always been there, but I had never thought much of it. Now, though, with my DNA test results staring back at me, it felt like a clue I had overlooked.

Aunt Anita's warning echoed in my head.

Stop looking.

But it was too late for that.

I needed answers.

I turned my focus to the DNA matches the test had given me.

The Stockstill name was nowhere to be found.

Instead, the strongest Y-DNA matches – distant relatives within four generations – had names I didn't recognize. Williams. Dixon.

I reached out to a few of them, carefully wording my messages, hoping someone could help.

Most didn't respond.

The ones who did had no idea who I was.

I spent nights at my laptop, eyes scanning endless family trees, trying to piece together connections that made no sense. Every lead ended in frustration. Every roadblock made my questions burn hotter.

Who was my father?

Why had my family never told me the truth?

Why had Aunt Anita been so adamant that I stop looking?

I wasn't just searching for a name. I was searching for myself.

And that kind of search doesn't stop just because someone tells you to.

It only makes you dig harder.

For most of my life, I had accepted that Jimmy Stockstill was my father. No matter how ugly that truth was, it was still a truth I had learned to live with. I didn't question it because I had no reason to. The people around me – my family, mother, and aunts – didn't tell me otherwise. And as a child, you trust that the adults in your life are telling you the truth.

Even as a kid, I was naturally curious and investigative. I remember being ten years old, a blonde-haired, blue-eyed boy, and wondering: Who is my father, really?

That curiosity eventually got the best of me.

One day, I pulled out the telephone book and began searching for the name "Stockstill". I felt a growing urge to know more. What started as innocent curiosity turned into determination.

Methodically, my tiny fingers started dialing the number of every Stockstill in the telephone directory. The responses varied. No answer. Busy signal. Other times, someone would answer only to say, "I don't know anyone with the name Jimmy Stockstill."

The calls were all the same. Dead ends. I was undeterred. I kept dialing.

I worked my way down the list and called the next number. It was listed to Jack Stockstill. I dialed. Someone answered!

"Hi, I'm Shannon Manley. I'm looking for Jimmy Stockstill. I think he might be my father."

Jack's reply came fast and cold: "Be thankful you don't know that asshole."

Click.

He hung up without another word.

The words hit me hard! Who was Jack Stockstill? And why was he so rude and abrupt?

Even after that curt, blunt response, I kept calling. Soon afterward, another call was answered.

"Hello," a woman said.

"Hi. My name is Shannon Manley. Do you know a Jimmy Stockstill?"

"I do," she replied.

My heart skipped, "I think he might be my father," I whispered quietly, trying to keep my composure.

Her name was Frances Stockstill – Jimmy's mother. I couldn't believe it. I thought I might be speaking to my paternal grandmother for the very first time.

I often wondered what might have been going through her head when she heard the sound of a ten-year-old boy whose childlike voice was still in its pre-puberty stage. Whatever she may have been thinking, Frances was kind, asked gentle questions, and seemed genuinely open to talking.

I learned that Jack, the man who hung up on my call, was Jimmy's father. Jack and Frances were divorced.

Frances stayed in touch with my mom and me for a while. She passed along messages between Jimmy and me – he was in prison at the time.

But looking back, there had been moments – fleeting, disjointed moments – that had planted tiny seeds of doubt. Things people said in passing. Comments that didn't make sense but weren't explained. I had brushed aside moments as a child, but they started to gnaw at me the older I got.

One of the first, most jarring moments came when I was a teenager.

I was snooping through my Aunt Anita's diary. I shouldn't have been – I knew that even then – but something about her private writings fascinated me. She was always so guarded, so careful with her words. But here, in these pages, she had written her raw, unfiltered thoughts. And that's when I saw it.

"I sure hope that Jimmy is the father and not the bastards who raped her."

I remember reading it repeatedly, the words blurring as my mind tried to process what I saw. It didn't make sense.

What did she mean? Did she hope Jimmy was my father? And what bastards? Who was she talking about?

At that moment, something cracked inside me. A fracture in the foundation of everything I had believed about myself. But I didn't ask Aunt Anita about it – not then. I was too afraid of what the answer might be.

Years later, when I was married, I brought it up. Casually. As if it were just some passing curiosity. I didn't want to make a big deal of it, even though, deep down, I already knew it was a big deal.

I asked her about what she had written.

She didn't react the way I expected. There was no hesitation, no moment of awkward denial. Instead, she went straight to her diary, tore the page out, and handed it to me. No words. No explanation. Just the torn paper, as if that action alone was supposed to answer my questions.

But it didn't. It only made them louder.

The doubts continued to build, little puzzle pieces that didn't quite fit together.

One of the most disturbing incidents happened when I was fifteen. I was eating lunch with Sybil at a restaurant called Casa Olé on Federal Road in East Houston. It was supposed to be a normal day, nothing unusual. But then, Sybil started acting strangely.

At first, it was subtle. She kept looking at me – staring, really – and something in her eyes made me uneasy. Her expression flickered between confusion and anger, and she seemed lost in thoughts she couldn't control. I had seen her like this before when her schizophrenia would take hold, but this time, it felt different.

Then, out of nowhere, she snapped.

She grabbed a container of salsa off the table and threw it at me. It hit my chest, splattering red across my white shirt, my lap, and the table. The people around us gasped, but I barely noticed them. All I could focus on was her voice, sharp and raw with rage.

"You look just like him! The man who raped me!"

The words hit me harder than the salsa ever could.

I sat there, frozen, watching as her face contorted with fury and something else – fear? Disgust? She started mumbling, incoherent words tumbling out in a frenzied mess as if she were arguing with someone who wasn't even there.

I had no idea what to do. People were staring. The waitress was hovering awkwardly nearby, unsure whether to intervene. I just wanted to disappear.

Sybil's outburst passed as quickly as it had come, but the damage was done.

I had always assumed that when she spoke about being raped, she was talking about Jimmy. That's what I had been led, or possibly chose to believe, my entire life. But now, with the DNA results in my hands and Sybil's words echoing in my mind, had I been wrong?

Was Jimmy my father?

Could it have been one of the men who raped my mother?

Throughout my childhood, my adoptive mother, Catherine, had a way of cutting me down in the cruelest ways. Her words were just as sharp as any blade. When she was angry, she didn't just punish me – she aimed for me, striking where it hurt the most.

"You're going to end up on the streets just like Sybil."

"You're going to end up like your father in prison."

"You are going to be a sexual pervert just like your father."

At the time, I thought she was talking about Jimmy. That was what made sense. He had been in and out of prison. He was on the sex offender registry – I had accepted the idea that I came from that kind of bloodline. But now, with everything I was learning, those words took on a new, even more horrifying meaning.

Was she talking about Jimmy?

Was she talking about someone else?

Growing up, I overheard her mention my father being in prison for rape more times than I could count. She would talk about Sybil's sexual assaults openly, in front of me, as if I wasn't there, as if the words weren't hitting me in the gut every time. I learned not to react. Not to ask questions. Because I had already learned, from a young age, that questions led to answers I wasn't ready to hear.

But now, I was ready.

And the truth was staring me right in the face.

The missing pieces were slowly falling into place, but one major question remained unanswered: If Jimmy Stockstill wasn't my father, then who was?

For years, I had pushed those doubts aside, convincing myself that I didn't need to know. But that changed in the early 2000s when I met Yessica Guzman.

She was my half-sister – or at least, that's what I thought. At the time, I had no reason to question it. Meeting her was supposed to be a moment of connection, a way to finally understand the other side of my family. But instead, it only deepened the mystery.

Yessica had traveled from Mexico to the United States in search of her father, Jimmy Stockstill. She had spent years trying to track him down, gathering every bit of information she could find. She had police records, arrest files, and pictures. She had done what I had never dared to do.

When she found me, I was excited. Thrilled, even. Finally, I had a connection to the other side of my family. A sister. Someone who shared my blood.

Or so I thought.

Meeting Yessica should have solidified the idea that Jimmy was my father. But instead, it did the opposite. Because as she told me everything she knew about him, something gnawed at me.

Her research was meticulous. She had records dating back decades, covering every period of his life and every place he had lived. But nowhere – nowhere – did my name appear.

If Jimmy were my father, wouldn't there be something? Some mention of me? Some proof?

Instead, all I had were warning signs.

A diary entry was torn out and handed to me in silence.

A schizophrenic mother throwing salsa and screaming words she had no control over.

An adoptive mother who wielded my father's crimes like a weapon against me.

And a sister who had spent years searching for her father – only to find that I wasn't part of his story at all.

Had I spent my whole life believing in a lie?

And now, piece by piece, the truth was beginning to surface.

Yessica was engaged to be married and invited me to her wedding in Dallas, Texas, on May 6, 2006. I was thrilled – not just for her but for what the wedding represented. It was an opportunity to meet more of my family, the people I had spent my life wondering about. My whole childhood had been a mess of whispered secrets and half-truths, but now, there was a chance to finally belong somewhere, to see the other side of my bloodline.

I had never met my father before. Not once. But that was about to change, too.

Jimmy Stockstill would be at the wedding.

I was twenty-six, and despite all the contradictions and strange comments about my paternity over the years, I still believed Jimmy was my father. I had questions, of course. Doubts. But what else was I supposed to believe? He was the only father I had ever had. I had never seen him, spoken to him, or even received a letter from him.

I wasn't sure how I expected that first meeting to go. Maybe a handshake, maybe an awkward hug, maybe some recognition in his eyes – like a man seeing his own face reflected in someone else's. I guess I imagined something like that, some kind of moment.

What I got was entirely different.

The reception was in full swing when I first laid eyes on him. Jimmy was slender and weathered, with an intensity about him that immediately put me on edge. He locked eyes with me from across the room, and before I could react, he was on me. He grabbed me by the shoulders, his fingers digging in tight like he thought he could hold me still, hold me in place.

His face twisted in anger, and then he shouted, "Not in my blood, boy! Not in my blood! No son of mine is going to be gay!"

And then, as if he could physically shake it out of me, he rattled my entire body like I was something defective that needed fixing.

The humiliation of that moment still lingers, the way the air seemed to freeze, the way people turned to stare. I remember the pressure of his hands, the spit flying from his mouth, and his alcohol drenched breath as he snarled those words at me. And most of all, I remember the sharp, searing realization that this was what I had spent twenty-six years waiting for.

This was my father.

That was the beginning and the end of any relationship I might have had with Jimmy Stockstill.

Over the years, I learned more about the kind of man Jimmy was. Not just homophobic but racist, too. He had been married before and had two sons from that marriage, but somewhere along the line, there had been bad business dealings, betrayals – whatever it was, they had completely cut him out of their lives.

He had lost everything, burned every bridge, and he was already alone by the time I met him.

In the fall of 2010, I got a call from an unfamiliar number. It was a hospice nurse. She told me that Jimmy was dying of cancer and wanted to see me.

I hesitated.

What did this man expect from me? We had never had a real conversation or a single moment of connection. And yet, here he was, calling for me when he had no one else left.

I don't know what made me do it – maybe curiosity, maybe some last remnant of that childhood desire to know him – but Joseph and I drove from Bryan, Texas, to Malakoff to see him.

It was jarring, seeing him like that. Weak. Frail. Nothing like the angry, snarling man who had tried to shake the gay out of me just four years earlier. He was hooked up to machines, his voice was thin, and I saw something human in him for the first time.

He asked me to be his medical power of attorney.

I should have said no.

But I didn't.

Jimmy and I started communicating again while his health was declining. It was during one of those conversations that he made a confession that shook me.

"I have always known that you were my son," Jimmy said, "but that mother of yours would have hung me for child support."

By this time, I had already received my DNA results, and I knew the Stockstill name didn't show up anywhere. There were warning signs. Something didn't add up. But his confession complicated things.

It wasn't just what he said, but how he said it. There was a quiet kind of certainty that made me question the science.

What if Jimmy had a different father? Maybe his father or a grandfather, who had been adopted a few generations back. That would explain why the name Stockstill didn't show up in my DNA results. Maybe I was grasping at straws. Was I trying too hard to reconcile Jimmy's confession and the family stories with the DNA results?

I was confused. With this new development and deathbed confession, there was part of me that still held on to the belief that he might be my birth father. For so many years, that had been my truth.

Jimmy died on January 16, 2011, at the age of 65.

There was no grand mourning, no outpouring of grief from long-lost loved ones. At the end of his life, the only family he had left to care for him were the two people he had spent his life resenting – a Hispanic daughter and a gay son.

That was the legacy he left behind.

On February 19, 2011, Yessica and I gathered a small group of our families in Galveston for a private ceremony on the beach. We honored him, not because of the man he was, but because of the man we had hoped he could have been.

Maybe, deep down, I had still been holding onto the idea that he was my father. Maybe, despite everything, I still wanted that to be true.

But the universe had other plans.

A few months after Jimmy's passing, Yessica ran into trouble.

Because she was born in Mexico, she needed to prove her citizenship to stay in the U.S. If she could verify that her biological father was Jimmy Stockstill, a U.S. citizen, she would be safe.

It seemed simple enough. We were siblings. At least, that was what we had always thought.

So, I agreed to take a DNA test with her.

We waited for the results. Days stretched into weeks. No part of me doubted what they would say.

Then, the results came in.

We were not siblings.

Not even close.

It hit like a sledgehammer to the chest. This wasn't just a mistake – this was irrefutable proof that one of us was not Jimmy's child.

And if Yessica wasn't my sister… that meant Jimmy Stockstill was not my father.

The next steps unfolded quickly. Yessica also contacted one of Jimmy's estranged sons and asked him to take a test. When his results came in, they confirmed what I already suspected: Yessica was Jimmy's biological daughter.

That left only one truth standing: Jimmy had never been my father.

Everything unraveled in an instant.

All the warnings, all the strange comments, all the gut feelings I had shoved down for years – they had been right.

The man I had spent my life believing in, searching for, hoping to connect with? He was a stranger.

And if he wasn't my father… then who was?

I went back to my DNA results with a vengeance, determined to uncover the truth about where I came from. No more false narratives, no more secrets.

For the first time in my life, I was ready to find out who I really was.

As soon as DNA had once again verified that Jimmy Stockstill was not my father, I was back to square one. I was so confused by all the stories I had heard, the warning signs that kept blaring like sirens, and now the hard, fast, and concrete evidence that once again brought more questions than answers.

For years, I had lived with a lie. The idea that I was Jimmy's son had shaped so much of my personal narrative. Even after I found out the truth about my mother and how I came to be, there was still some strange comfort in thinking I had at least one certain connection. But I didn't.

There were moments when I tried to push it out of my mind. Maybe the truth didn't matter. Maybe it was better to leave the past alone and stop chasing answers that only seemed to bring more chaos. But the thing about truth is that it doesn't go away just because you ignore it. It lingers, whispers, and makes itself known in ways you don't expect.

The night terrors that had haunted me for as long as I could remember came back worse than ever.

I have suffered from night terrors on and off throughout my entire life. Perhaps this was from some unknown, unidentified trauma in my childhood. Periodically, the terrors would be so bad that I would wake up in the middle of the night screaming at the top of my lungs. Sometimes, I would run through the house. On a few occasions during these episodes, I would actually run out of the house, down flights of stairs, and into the street.

One constant throughout the night terrors is that I would have no recollection of them. I wouldn't remember specifics of what happened. The next day, I would usually sense that I had experienced one because I would wake up very tired. During the night terrors, my heart rate would race to over 200 beats per minute. I would also be sore the next morning because my muscles were tense during the episodes. I could only confirm I had a night of terror by someone confirming the event and relating the details of what transpired.

After learning all this new information and realizing that Jimmy was not my father, the night terrors intensified.

Joseph and I were living in a small apartment in Bryan, Texas, during this time. One night, I woke up screaming at the top of my lungs and started running through the apartment. Joseph managed to tackle me right before I opened the front door and managed to get me back to bed safely.

Once again, I did not remember any details of this event until Joseph relayed them to me the next morning. Later in the day, I saw one of our neighbors who lived next door, who asked me, "Did you hear that last night? It sounded like someone was getting murdered!"

I quietly smiled and responded, "No. I didn't hear anything."

I didn't know how to explain it. I barely understood it myself. But it was getting worse.

I tried to rationalize it. Maybe it was just stress. A biological response to the constant upheaval in my life. But part of me knew better. It felt like something deep inside me was fighting to get out – something that had been buried for a long time.

I had spent years wondering why I had these episodes. I wondered why I carried this strange, unexplainable tension inside me. As a child, I had brushed it off as bad dreams. As a teenager, I assumed it was anxiety. But this was something else. This was something bigger than me, something I couldn't control.

And now, with everything I had learned, it was becoming harder and harder to ignore the fact that my body might be remembering something my mind had long since buried.

But what? Could it have been inherited trauma?

I kept replaying everything in my head. Every conversation. Every warning sign. The way both my biological and adoptive mothers refused to talk about my father. The way my aunt got so defensive whenever I asked questions. I had spent my entire life believing in one story, only for DNA to prove – twice – that it was false.

I felt like I was unraveling.

For so long, I had tried to be a good nephew. I had tried to respect my aunt's wishes. I owed her that. But at the same time, I owed myself the truth.

I had thought Jimmy was my father. That had turned out to be a lie.

I had thought Yessica was my half-sister. That had turned out to be a lie.

How many more lies had I been told?

And if Jimmy wasn't my father, then who was?

I started obsessing over my DNA results again. I spent hours combing through records, cross-referencing names, trying to find even the smallest connection that might give me a lead.

It became an addiction. A relentless, unyielding hunger for answers.

I stopped sleeping.

When I did manage to fall asleep, I was plagued by dreams that left me feeling uneasy – dark, shapeless things that I couldn't quite grasp but knew were there.

My world had narrowed to a single goal: Find the truth.

Every time I thought I was getting close, I would hit another dead end.

I reached out to people I had never met before – distant relatives, old acquaintances, anyone who might know something. Some were helpful. Most weren't. Some seemed genuinely confused when I asked them about my father, as if they had never heard of him.

And that was the strangest part.

If Jimmy Stockstill wasn't my father, then who was? Why didn't anyone seem to know?

I kept thinking about Sybil and the way she had always changed the subject whenever I asked about my father.

Was she protecting me?

Or was she protecting herself?

One night, it all came to a head when I sat on the couch, staring at my laptop screen, exhausted, frustrated, desperate.

I had spent years trying to put this puzzle together. I had found pieces. I had connected with some of them. But the picture still didn't make sense.

And for the first time in my life, I realized I was afraid of the answer.

Because what if the truth was worse than the lie?

What if I wasn't ready for it?

I closed my laptop and leaned back, staring at the ceiling. My mind was racing, but I was too tired to keep going.

Joseph sat down beside me, silent for a long time before speaking.

"You're gonna drive yourself crazy with this," he said.

I let out a short, humorless laugh, "I think I already have."

He sighed, "Maybe you should take a break."

"I can't."

"Why?"

Because I needed to know. Because I had to know. Because I couldn't keep living like this, haunted by questions that had no answers.

But I didn't say that.

Instead, I just shook my head.

Joseph didn't push. He just reached for my hand and squeezed it.

And for a moment, I let myself breathe.

For a moment, I let myself rest. But deep down, I knew this wasn't over. I had come too far to stop now. And whether I was ready for it or not, the truth was out there.

Waiting for me.

At this point, I had realized that Jimmy Stockstill was not my father. That much was clear. What wasn't clear was why everyone seemed so desperate to keep me from finding out who he really was.

I had grown up being told one thing, only to have it shattered by DNA results – twice. There was no more room for doubt. No more space for excuses. I had been lied to.

The question now was: Why?

And more importantly – by whom?

I could still hear Aunt Anita's voice in my head, her urgent tone, her pleading words.

You don't need to keep looking, Shannon. Just let it go.

But how could I?

If this was just some harmless mistake – some simple case of misidentification – why was she so adamant that I stop searching? Why did she sound afraid?

Because if there was nothing to hide, why all the secrecy?

It wasn't just Aunt Anita. Other relatives had started acting differently, dodging my questions, brushing off my concerns, and offering vague reassurances that I "didn't need to dig any deeper."

But I did.

I wasn't asking for permission anymore.

I didn't care who it upset.

For as long as I could remember, I had wanted answers about my past. But this wasn't just curiosity anymore. This wasn't some lingering childhood question that I could shrug off and move on from.

This was my life. This was my identity. And I had every right to know the truth.

If Jimmy Stockstill wasn't my father, then someone else was. Someone who had been deliberately kept from me. Someone whose very existence had been erased from my history.

I wasn't going to stop until I found him. Because the deeper I looked, the more it became clear – this wasn't just about uncovering a name. It was about uncovering a secret. A secret that had been buried for a reason, something that people were afraid of.

But I wasn't afraid.

Not anymore.

I was ready to find the truth.

No matter what it was.

No matter what it cost me.

Chapter 3: The Brutal Truth

I had been searching for my father. That was all I had wanted – a name, a face, some sense of where I came from. But what I found instead was something much darker.

It was one of my mother's first cousins who finally told me. Unlike Aunt Anita, who had only given me vague warnings and pleaded with me to stop digging, this cousin came right out with it. There was no hesitation, no sugarcoating. She was straightforward, almost clinical, as if she had been waiting for someone to ask the right questions for years.

"Your mother was raped brutally," she told me, "left for dead."

My breath caught in my throat.

I had prepared myself for the possibility that my father was someone Sybil hadn't wanted to remember. I had considered the idea that maybe she had gotten pregnant by accident or that it was the result of a short-lived relationship.

But this? This was something else entirely.

The cousin kept talking, her voice steady, like she was reciting facts from a police report rather than telling me the most horrifying truth of my life.

"It happened on October 30, 1978," she said. "Three men attacked her. It wasn't random. They planned it. And they nearly killed her."

My heart pounded as I absorbed her words. The image forming in my mind was too much to process – my mother, just twenty-five years old, was beaten, violated, and left for dead.

I tried to ask something, anything, but my throat felt like it had closed up. The cousin must have sensed the shock on the other end of the phone line because she softened just slightly.

"She was in the hospital for weeks," she said. "They didn't think she would make it."

It made sense now – why Sybil never spoke about my father, why so many people had told me to let it go, why I had always felt like there was something about my origins that no one wanted to talk about.

It wasn't just a secret.

It was a crime.

A brutal, violent crime.

And somehow, in the aftermath of that horror, I had been conceived.

I don't remember how I ended the conversation. I don't remember saying goodbye or hanging up the phone. All I remember is the way my stomach twisted as I tried to make sense of what I had just learned.

For years, I had imagined my father as a man with a story – maybe one who had been young and irresponsible or someone who had walked away before he even knew Sybil was pregnant. But now, I wasn't searching for a man.

I was searching for a rapist.

Maybe three of them.

I had spent months tracing my DNA, connecting dots, following leads. Now, none of that seemed to matter. What I needed wasn't hidden in genealogy records. It was buried in something much darker – police reports, hospital records, evidence of a crime that had shaped my very existence. That was the only way to know for sure. I had to see it with my own eyes. I had to find the records.

I started with the hospital.

If Sybil had been hospitalized after the attack, there had to be records. Medical records don't just disappear. Someone, somewhere, had to have a file that documented what had happened to her.

I expected resistance. I knew that the odds of finding anything were slim after nearly thirty-five years. But I had to try.

I spent hours on the phone, calling hospital administrators and explaining what I was looking for without revealing too much. I knew that if I mentioned the word "rape," there was a chance they would shut me down. But when I framed it as a search for my mother's old medical records – documents that might help me understand my health history – I found people who were willing to listen.

One call led to another. One dead end turned into a new lead. I followed every thread, no matter how thin, refusing to let go of the idea that there was proof of what had happened somewhere in an old file room.

And then, finally, I found it.

A woman in the records department confirmed it over the phone.

"Yes, we have the records."

I froze.

I had spent so long searching, preparing myself for disappointment, that I hadn't actually considered what it would feel like to hear those words.

"Are you sure?" I asked.

She paused, checking something in the system, "Yes. There's a file here. It's archived, but it hasn't been destroyed."

I felt my breath shake as I exhaled.

This was real.

This wasn't just family whispers or vague warnings. This was documented, recorded, and buried in a file that had been sitting untouched for decades.

And I was about to see it.

The day I picked up the file, I sat in my car for a long time before opening it. The envelope felt heavy in my hands. I wasn't sure if I was ready. I had wanted answers, but now that they were right in front of me, I felt sick.

What if the details were worse than I imagined? What if seeing them in writing made it impossible to ever unsee them?

But I had come too far to stop now.

With shaking hands, I tore the envelope open.

The first thing I saw was my mother's name. Her birthdate. The date of admission.

October 30, 1978.

I swallowed hard.

I flipped to the next page.

And there it was – everything.

A list of injuries. Multiple contusions. Internal trauma. Signs of prolonged assault. The words blurred in front of me as I tried to process them.

She had been beaten unconscious.

She had suffered broken ribs, a fractured cheekbone, and internal bleeding.

She had almost died.

I clenched my jaw, gripping the pages so tightly my knuckles turned white. This wasn't just some old rumor. This was real. This was what had happened to my mother. And this was how I had come into the world.

The next step was finding the police report.

If she had been hospitalized, there would have had to be a police record. Someone had to have investigated the crime. Someone had to have known what happened.

I spent weeks tracking it down. Calling precincts, filing requests, hitting roadblocks at every turn.

While I was never able to locate or obtain a formal police report, an incident report was documented in the medical records.

Three men.

A planned attack.

They had watched her. Followed her. Waited for the right moment.

They had dragged her into an abandoned park.

They had left her there, bleeding and unconscious, assuming she wouldn't survive.

But she had.

And she had given birth to me. I sat with the file in my lap, staring at the words. My whole life, I had wanted to know where I came from. Now I knew. And I didn't know what to do with it.

The more I dug into the past, the more the pieces of my mother's life came together. Each detail painted a clearer picture, but it was not one I wanted to see. It was raw, horrifying, and impossible to erase from my mind. Every word on those reports cemented the truth I was struggling to grasp.

According to the medical records, on the night of October 29, 1978, Sybil got into a car with three men. There was no way to determine if she had been seeking a ride or if they had lured her in with false kindness. Either way, what followed was nothing short of a nightmare. The reports didn't list the names of the perpetrators; they were just three unidentified males. They had taken her somewhere secluded, where no one could hear her scream, where no one would come to help.

The next entry in the report was clinical, devoid of emotion, just a recounting of injuries. It stated she had been found by a concerned citizen in the early morning hours of October 30, 1978. She was in duress and a confused state – bruised, beaten, battered, and sexually assaulted. Jesse and Pearl Spence, her uncle and aunt, received a phone call from the authorities who told them that Sybil was in bad shape and needed help. No other details were given; she was alone and outside, and it did not make sense.

When they found her, she was barely recognizable. Her face was swollen, bruises darkening the delicate skin around her eyes. A cut split her lower lip, and her dress was torn and stained with dirt. The report noted that she had injuries consistent with being struck multiple times, abrasions on her wrists and arms, and defensive wounds, meaning she had tried to fight back. That part haunted me the most – knowing she had resisted and that she had tried to stop them, but they had overpowered her.

The description of the assault was brief, reduced to sterile terminology meant to categorize and document rather than convey the horror of what had happened to her. "Vaginal and anal trauma consistent with sexual assault." That was all it said. A cold, detached statement that somehow carried the weight of everything I never wanted to know.

The report continued, explaining that Jesse and Pearl immediately took Sybil to the hospital. She was in a state of confusion, unable to recall everything clearly. She could barely speak, her voice hoarse, her responses disjointed. The nurses noted her erratic behavior, the way she flinched at sudden movements, the way she kept rubbing her arms as if trying to rid herself of something unseen.

After being treated for her physical injuries, she was transferred to the Harris County Psychiatric Hospital for observation. The decision was made quickly. The doctors noted that she was exhibiting signs of paranoia and extreme distress. She kept insisting that someone was watching her and that they were coming back for her. She refused to eat at times, muttering to herself, clutching the hospital blanket as if it were the only thing keeping her grounded.

By November 9, 1978, a court order had been issued, committing her to Austin State Hospital for not exceeding ninety days. The records stated that she was being admitted for evaluation and treatment, though even then, there was little optimism about her long-term prognosis.

It was during this hospitalization that her diagnosis became official – paranoid schizophrenia.

It felt impossible to separate what had happened to her from what came after. Had the attack triggered her schizophrenia? Or had it already been present, only made worse by the trauma? The doctors couldn't say for sure, but one thing was certain: my mother was never the same after that night.

And that's when the second devastating truth was uncovered. She was pregnant.

It was noted in the records as a routine finding, just another medical fact in a long list of details. But to me, it was the moment that changed everything.

The first trimester. That's how early they caught it. She was carrying a child, the product of that night.

Me.

I read that line over and over again, my vision blurring, my breath catching in my throat. It was real. It wasn't just an ugly possibility or a rumor whispered among relatives. It was documented, written down, and recorded in black and white.

The reports didn't say how she reacted to the news. I wondered if she even understood. If, in her fragile mental state, she could grasp what was happening. Or if it had simply been another weight added to an already unbearable burden.

No one in my family ever talked about what happened in those months following her attack. If they knew she was pregnant and were aware of the circumstances, they never spoke of it. Maybe they thought they were protecting her. Or maybe, deep down, they knew the truth was too painful to confront.

I tried to imagine what it was like for her. Locked away in that hospital, surrounded by strangers in white coats, her mind fractured, her body still healing. Did she ever hold her stomach, wondering about the life inside her? Did she ever feel a moment of love for me, or was I just another cruel reminder of what had been stolen from her?

The medical records couldn't answer those questions. They only provided facts. She remained at Austin State Hospital for the full ninety days. She returned to the Roark household when she was released, where her Uncle Sherrill and Aunt Catherine took her in. But the woman they brought back was not the same one who had left.

She had become unpredictable. Some days, she would sit in silence for hours, staring at nothing, lost in a world no one else could see. On other days, she was frantic, pacing the house, talking to herself, and making wild accusations about people trying to harm her.

Sherrill and Catherine tried their best to care for her, but they were ill-equipped to handle her condition. Psychiatric care was limited, and mental illness was still deeply misunderstood. Due to her pregnancy, she had been removed from her psychiatric medications, which only exacerbated her symptoms.

By the time she gave birth to me, she had already begun to slip further away.

I thought about the life she could have had. About the person she might have been if that night had never happened. Would she have finished school? Would she have found love and built a family on her own terms? Or was this always going to be her fate?

I would never know. All I had were these records, these fragments of a story that had been kept from me for so long.

I closed the file, but the words remained burned into my memory. My mother was never able to fully recover.

And in some ways, I wasn't sure if I ever would either.

Learning the truth about my mother's past altered something inside me. It was one thing to grow up not knowing the full details of my origins, but it was another to have them laid out in front of me in black and white. The reality of my existence was now tied to an act of unimaginable violence, and no matter how much I tried to rationalize it, I couldn't escape the weight of that fact. It was like carrying a ghost – one that lingered in my mind, whispering reminders of a history I never asked for.

In the days following my discovery, I felt an overwhelming sense of anxiety. I would wake up in the middle of the night, my heart pounding and my thoughts racing. I would think about Sybil in that hospital, broken and lost, and wonder how she had managed to survive. I would think about the faceless men who had done this to her, walking free, unpunished, nameless shadows that had dictated the course of both of our lives. The frustration of it all clawed at me relentlessly.

It wasn't just that they had hurt her. It was that they had gotten away with it.

The reports I read confirmed what I had feared. There had been no real investigation. The police had taken down the details, documented her injuries, and left it at that. An incident report had been filed, but that was all. There was no evidence that a case had ever been opened, no indication that officers had pursued her attackers, no notes about follow-ups, and no witness statements. It was as if Sybil had been deemed unworthy of justice before the ink on the paperwork had even dried.

That thought sickened me.

She had been brutalized, discarded, and left to pick up the pieces of her shattered life, while the men who did this to her continued living theirs without consequence. They had stolen something from her – her safety, her trust, her sanity – and the system had allowed them to walk away.

I tried to put myself in her shoes, to understand how she must have felt waking up in that hospital, knowing that no one was coming to make it right. Was she even surprised?

Had she expected justice? Or had she already known, deep down, that women like her didn't get justice?

The more I thought about it, the angrier I became at the world that had let this happen.

The world that had failed to protect her, failed to hold them accountable, and, in many ways, failed me, too.

Their actions didn't just end with her. They created me. They forced her to carry something she never should have had to carry.

I struggled with that thought more than anything else.

Did she ever look at her growing belly and feel resentment? Did she ever press a hand against her stomach and wish it would all go away?

I wouldn't have blamed her if she did. I don't think I could have done it if I had been in her position. I don't think I could have survived it.

And yet, she did.

She endured nine months of carrying me, reliving that night with every change in her body. She went through labor, went through the pain of delivery, knowing exactly where I had come from.

And I had to ask myself: Was I just another wound? Another scar left behind by men who had already taken too much?

The sadness of it all settled deep in my bones.

I wished I could have gone back in time, found her before any of this happened, warned her, and protected her. I wished I could have erased that night, not just for her but for myself. I didn't want to be tied to this story. I didn't want my existence to be tangled up in violence and suffering.

But no amount of wishing could change what had already happened.

For days, I carried that knowledge like a sickness. I walked around with an ache, a hollowness I couldn't explain. I had always known that Sybil struggled with her mental health, but now, I understood why. Now, I saw the full picture, and it devastated me.

The trauma of that night had never left her. It had followed her, haunted her, consumed her.

And I had been part of that trauma.

It wasn't just that she had been assaulted. She had been forced to live with the reminder of it growing inside her daily.

She had been forced to give birth to the child of her rapists.

To me.

That thought was unbearable.

I had to wonder – did giving birth to me break her even more? Did she see my face and feel only pain? Did she ever love me at all?

There was no way to know for sure.

I wanted to believe that, in some way, despite everything, there had been moments of love. Maybe there were times when she held me and felt something other than sorrow. Maybe there were fleeting instances where she saw me not as a product of her pain but as something separate from it.

But I couldn't lie to myself.

I couldn't ignore the reality of what she had endured.

She had never fully recovered. That much was clear.

And now, I wasn't sure if I would either.

I found myself questioning everything I had ever believed about my own life. Despite her struggles, I had always assumed that Sybil had wanted me somehow. That she had chosen to keep me. But now, I realized she hadn't been given a choice at all.

The decision had been made for her the moment she was left bleeding and broken on that street. I had always seen myself as a person separate from her pain, but that was impossible. I was tied to it. I was born from it.

And that fact sat heavily on my chest, an unbearable weight I didn't know how to carry.

For the first time, I felt like a walking reminder of something monstrous.

I wasn't just a person. I was the evidence of a crime. A crime that had never been solved, something that had never even been investigated. And the men who did it? They were out there somewhere. Maybe dead, maybe still alive, maybe living quiet lives with their own families, their own children, unaware – or perhaps indifferent – to the destruction they had left behind.

The thought made my stomach turn.

I wanted justice, but it was decades too late. The police had failed Sybil in 1978, and there was no way they would do anything about it now. No DNA evidence, no names, and no leads. Just a case that had never really existed in the first place.

I had never felt so powerless.

I knew I couldn't change the past. I knew I couldn't go back and fix what had been broken. But I also knew I couldn't let this story end in silence.

Sybil had never gotten justice.

Seeing my mother's mental illness through the lens of what she endured forced me to see her in a way I never had before. For most of my life, I had only known the version of Sybil, who had been lost to paranoia, the one whose mind had betrayed her, the one who was incapable of being a mother to me.

I had lived with the reality of her absence, with the consequences of her neglect, with the ache of not having a mother to guide me. But now, with the weight of these new discoveries pressing down on me, I realized I had never truly known her.

Sybil hadn't failed as a mother – she had never even had a chance to be one.

Before the attack, she had been a functioning adult, navigating life as best as she could, trying to survive despite the difficult hand she had been dealt. But after that night, she was never the same. The brutal assault didn't just leave her physically wounded; it shattered something inside of her, something that could never be put back together. What was left of Sybil after that night was only fragments of the woman she had once been.

I had spent years wondering why she hadn't been able to care for me, why she had let me go. I had carried resentment toward her, even when I knew she had struggled with her mental health. But now, as I pored over her medical records, the truth was staring me in the face. Sybil had been utterly destroyed.

She had been twenty-five years old – just a young woman – when three men took everything from her. She was beaten so severely that her body bore the evidence of their violence. She was raped and left for dead, and when she was found, she was so battered that she was barely recognizable. The damage was irreversible, both physically and mentally. The attack hadn't just left scars; it had rewritten the very foundation of who she was.

And one of those men – one of those monsters – was possibly my biological father.

That fact would never stop haunting me.

I sat with that information for what felt like an eternity. It was one thing to know I had come into this world as a result of something violent, but it was another thing entirely to know that the person who had fathered me may have been directly responsible for my mother's suffering. How was I supposed to reconcile that? How was I supposed to make peace with the fact that half of my DNA came from a man capable of such brutality?

The weight of it was suffocating.

As I read on, the records painted an even more tragic picture of Sybil's life long before that night in 1978.

She had been born a twin – one of two girls brought into the world on June 6, 1953. Sybil and Anita. Two sisters, bound together from the very beginning. But their childhood was far from idyllic. Their mother, Myrtle Morris Tennyson, had abandoned them when they were still babies.

Abandoned.

That word caught in my throat.

For two weeks, no one knew where Myrtle had gone. She simply left, vanishing from their lives without a trace. And when the twins were finally found, they were in conditions too horrifying to comprehend. They were filthy, covered in grime, and worse – roaches were crawling all over their tiny bodies.

The image of it made my stomach turn. Two helpless babies, left in filth and neglect, their cries unanswered.

It was a miracle they had even survived.

After that, they were taken in by their grandmother and later placed in their father's and paternal grandparents' custody. But the damage had already been done. The trauma of abandonment doesn't just fade – it burrows deep, shaping the way a person sees the world and the way they see themselves.

How could Sybil have ever felt safe after that?

How could she have ever believed that people wouldn't leave her?

Her life had been marked by loss and suffering from the very beginning.

And it didn't stop there.

The medical records revealed something even darker, making my breath catch in my chest.

Sybil had suffered from prior sexual assaults from an early age.

She had been violated long before that night in 1978. Long before she was old enough even to understand what was happening to her.

And suddenly, everything made sense.

She had dropped out of school in the ninth grade. She had struggled in ways no child should have to. She had spent her entire life in survival mode, trying to escape the horrors that had been forced upon her.

By the time she was twenty-five, the attack that led to my conception wasn't the beginning of her suffering – it was just another chapter in an already tragic story.

A story that no one had ever stopped to truly see.

A story that had been buried, ignored, forgotten.

I sat there, gripping the records, my hands shaking.

Sybil had never been given a chance.

Not as a child. Not as a teenager. Not as a young woman.

She had been born into a world that failed to protect her. And when she needed help the most and someone to fight for her, the world turned its back on her again.

No wonder she never recovered.

No wonder she descended into paranoia, into schizophrenia.

Her mind had been fractured by years of trauma, by years of unspeakable pain. The attack in 1978 wasn't the first thing to break her – it was simply the final thing she couldn't survive.

And now, I understood.

I understood why she had let me go.

I understood why she had never been able to care for Christy, my older half-sister.

She wasn't just a mentally ill woman who had failed as a mother. She was a woman who had been broken long before she even had the chance to be one.

She never got to be just a person.

Her entire life had been defined by the suffering others inflicted upon her.

And that realization hit me harder than anything else.

I had spent so much of my life wondering why she hadn't been capable of loving me, why she hadn't been capable of raising me. And now, I saw the answer staring back at me in black and white.

It was never about me.

It was never about anything I did or didn't do.

Sybil had never been given the tools to care for anyone, not even herself.

She had been raised in neglect. She had been subjected to violence. She had been tossed aside and left to fend for herself before she even had the chance to know what safety felt like. She was never allowed to heal.

And without healing, how could she have possibly been expected to be a mother?

I swallowed the lump in my throat, staring down at the records, feeling like I was finally seeing my mother for the first time.

Not as the unstable woman who had been absent from my life.

Not as the mother who had failed me.

But as a person.

As a woman who had been through hell and never found her way back.

And I realized something at that moment. I had spent years looking for answers. And now that I had them, I didn't know what to do with them. All I knew was that I would never see Sybil the same way again.

Chapter 4: The Hunt Begins

Once I had confirmation that Jimmy Lee Stockstill was not my biological father, everything shifted. The identity I had accepted for years seemed to crack down the center, and the pieces scattered into a thousand possibilities. I remember sitting with the DNA report from FamilyTreeDNA.

It was short, clinical, and final.

"No recognizable match."

There was no emotion in those words, but I sure felt the weight of what they meant. Jimmy Lee wasn't my father. And just like that, I was back at square one – but with a fire in me I hadn't felt in years.

In the spring of 2012, the hunt had officially begun.

I returned to my DNA matches, poring over names and noting anything that might suggest a connection. Back then, things were different. Autosomal DNA testing – the kind that can tell you about relationships across all family lines – was just being introduced into genetic genealogy and was not well utilized. The only tool I had at my disposal was Y-DNA. It traced the direct male lineage. And even with its limitations, it offered me one thing I didn't have before: a clue.

There was one match that stood out.

A man with the last name Williams. We matched on 37 markers, which, in 2010, was considered a strong Y-DNA match within four generations. That single connection became my starting point. Everything from that moment on revolved around the name Williams. I started building out family trees. I traced branches forward and backward, filled notebooks with names and dates, created folders on my desktop with cross-referenced files, and saved everything twice. I didn't have a clear direction, but I knew I had to chase this thread with everything I had.

It turned out the Williams family was rooted in Evergreen, Alabama – a small town with a deep southern history. As I studied the family's lineage, something started to feel strangely familiar. Some members of the Williams family were Pentecostal – just like me, just like the environment both Joseph and I had grown up in.

From there, I went into research overdrive. I searched through census records, church directories, obituaries, and online forums. I called libraries in Alabama and pulled every historical record I could get my hands on. I began contacting people – distant cousins, even people with no known relationship but who happened to carry the Williams surname.

Some were kind, others confused, and a few didn't bother responding at all. I understood. After all, I was asking questions that could unearth things most families prefer to leave buried.

Still, I pressed on.

I spent weeks – months, honestly – trying to determine which branch of the Williams family could have ended up in Texas in 1978. I had to find someone who would've been in Houston at the time of Sybil's attack. Someone who fits the profile. I started with the obvious. Military transfers. Job relocations. College enrollments. I checked voter registrations, tax records, property deeds – anything that might tie a Williams man to Southeast Texas at that particular time.

Eventually, I struck something that looked promising.

One branch of the Williams family had migrated from Alabama to Texas well before the 70s. Two names stood out immediately – Oscar Wise Williams and Walter Lee Williams. Oscar had moved to Vidor, Texas, where he opened a bar.

A bar owner in Southeast Texas during the '60s?

That piqued my interest. It was enough of a lead to dig deeper.

But almost just as quickly as I found it, the lead fell apart. Oscar had passed away in 1964. That was fourteen years before I was even conceived. He had no sons, only one daughter. Just like that, I had to cross him off the list.

It was a hard hit.

For a few days, I let myself feel the disappointment. I had allowed myself to hope and imagine that maybe the search would end sooner than expected. But I learned pretty quickly in this process that genealogy wasn't a straight path – it was a winding road with more dead ends than open doors.

Still, even though Oscar was ruled out, his connection to the area kept me digging into that particular branch of the family. If Oscar had relocated, maybe others had too. Maybe someone younger – a nephew, a cousin – had followed the same path. The Williams family was large. Dozens of branches, hundreds of names. I started mapping out each one, trying to account for every male who was of reproductive age in 1978 and had a plausible link to Southeast Texas.

That left me looking at one other line within the Williams family tree that hadn't yet been fully explored – Walter Lee Williams. Walter wasn't someone I had originally considered, but the more I uncovered, the more he rose to the surface as someone worth investigating. He had lived in Houston in the late '70s and owned a small business in the area. His name popped up in local directories from that time, and I began reaching out to anyone I could find connected to him.

The relatives I contacted painted a mostly positive picture of Walter. He was described as hardworking, married, present, and devoted to his family.

"A good man."

"Always there for his kids."

But occasionally, a different tone would surface in the conversations. A few family members made comments that stood out – not accusatory or dramatic, just carefully worded hints.

"There were times in his life," one relative told me, "where I wouldn't be surprised if he had fathered another child. He was just that kind of man. Not a bad person, just... complicated."

That was all I needed to hear. In a search like mine, words like "complicated" and "wouldn't be surprised" were like neon signs. I didn't assume anything, but I couldn't ignore them either.

Walter became a potential father.

He also had two sons, both of whom would've been old enough in 1978 to potentially be my biological father. I started with the one I could reach first – Donald Vernon Williams, who went by Don. After some digging, I managed to get in contact with him. I told him who I was, what I had learned, and what I hoped to find out. He listened carefully. There was no defensiveness, no resistance. Just honest curiosity.

Don was confident he couldn't be my father. He didn't hesitate or seem unsure. He explained where he had been and what he had been doing during that time in 1978, and his story lined up. But Don didn't stop there.

He offered something unexpected – a lead.

He told me about a cousin who had been in the Houston area during the late 1970s. Someone named Douglas Lamar

Williams, or Doug, as most people called him. It was the first time I'd heard Doug's name. Until then, he hadn't appeared in any of my research, and I had no prior knowledge of him.

According to Don, Doug had experienced some trouble back in Alabama and moved to Houston to be closer to family. That immediately made him a person of interest.

The timeline fit.

The location fit. And thanks to Don's willingness to talk, I had a new path to follow.

Don didn't hesitate to share what he knew. In fact, he offered to help me get in contact with Doug himself. It was rare to find someone who was so open, and I appreciated it deeply.

Around that same time, I made another connection – Gordon Johnson. Gordon's mother had been one of Walter Lee Williams's daughters. That made Gordon a grandson of Walter. When I reached out to him, he was more than happy to help. He didn't have all the answers, but he was generous with what he did know. He talked about family history, shared names and stories, and offered to check with relatives who might have more information.

Gordon told me something that struck me in a very personal way.

"You know," he said, "my mother was the family historian. She kept every record, every birthday, every marriage certificate. She would've loved to talk to you.

Would've had a hundred questions and probably a few answers, too. I wish she were still around. She'd have been fascinated by all of this."

It was one of those small but meaningful moments that reminded me how much this search was about more than just DNA. It was about connections, both lost and found. I thanked Gordon and added his input to the growing file of information I'd accumulated over the last several months on the Williams family.

With Don ruled out, Walter still a possibility, and Gordon helping me explore the wider family, I decided to reach out to the last name left on my immediate list – Doug.

I found a phone number for him and decided to call. My heart was pounding when he picked up. I introduced myself and gave him a brief overview of who I was and why I was calling. Doug didn't interrupt. He didn't get defensive. He listened, and when I finished, he paused for a long moment before responding.

"I'm sorry," he said, "but it's impossible. I was in prison at the time. There's no way I could be your father."

It was a clear answer, yet it didn't end the conversation. Doug didn't hang up. In fact, he seemed more curious than anything. He asked me questions. He wanted to know more about me, the DNA match, my life, and my search. We talked for a while, and by the end of the conversation, Doug invited me and Joseph to meet him in person for lunch. I accepted immediately.

Even though Doug had denied being my father, I couldn't help but feel excited. This was the first time I was going to meet someone from the Williams family who was directly connected to my Y-DNA line. Even if he wasn't the one, he knew things. He remembered people. He could help me trace connections. It felt like I was moving – real, tangible movement in a search that had often felt stalled.

That didn't rule him out of my Y-DNA match, though. It only ruled him out as a direct father. The connection was still there. Doug and I shared a common male ancestor – someone upstream in the Williams line.

I had already spoken to Don, who had firmly ruled himself out. That left his brother and their father as the two remaining possibilities. And while Walter had passed away in 1987, his timeline still placed him in the right area at the right time. That made him the oldest possibility, but not an unlikely one. Depending on his age and life circumstances in 1978, it was still possible he could be my father.

From a DNA standpoint, the only thing that would tell me more would be additional tests – more data points. If I could convince other family members to test, especially from Walter's line, I could start to triangulate the connection more precisely. But getting people to test was never easy. Some were willing, others were hesitant, and a few flat-out refused. I understood. But I couldn't help but feel that the answer was now orbiting just around that small group of names.

At that point in my search, I had a clearer picture than ever before. I had the right surname. I had the Y-DNA match. I had the geographic location. I had three possible men in the same family – one father and two sons – who could all potentially be the missing piece.

Don seemed confident that Doug was just another relative living in Houston at the right time. But something about Doug kept pulling me back. I hadn't met him yet, but I could sense that he might be the missing link. I didn't want to move forward on guesses or hunches. I needed proof – clarity. And I wasn't going to get that by sitting still. So, I decided to look deeper into Doug.

I started a more detailed dive into his background. I wanted to know exactly who I was dealing with. That's when I uncovered a critical piece of information that shifted everything. Doug was on the sex offender registry. That alone sent a chill through me. But it also meant there were public records available. So, I kept going.

I found arrest records. I found documentation related to criminal charges. I located his prison record and paid close attention to the dates. Doug had told me – firmly – that he had been in prison during the time I was conceived. That was the reason he couldn't possibly be my father.

It was a clear alibi.

One that should have ruled him out completely.

But it didn't.

According to the official records, Doug was not incarcerated in October 1978 – the month Sybil was attacked. That detail alone changed everything. His alibi wasn't just shaky; it was incorrect. He wasn't where he said he was.

Suddenly, Doug couldn't be ruled out. I had to add him to the list of possibilities. And that list of men in the Williams family who could have been my potential father was growing.

Joseph and I arranged to meet Doug in person. I wanted to talk to him face to face – to get a sense of who he was, to look him in the eye, and maybe, just maybe, get answers I couldn't find in a file or a database.

We chose a small restaurant called Taqueria Abasolo on Hogan Road in Houston. It was located right next to Doug's apartment, which made it convenient for him. It was a warm day, the kind of day where everything feels a little heavier and slower. Joseph and I left Bryan, Texas, that morning with a mixture of anticipation and anxiety. We didn't know what to expect; we just knew we needed to go. I didn't go into that meeting with any specific expectations. I just wanted to meet him, talk face-to-face, and gather whatever I could.

Doug walked into the restaurant wearing a fitted white t-shirt, black shorts, white tube socks pulled up to his knees, and sandals. His appearance was casual but deliberate. He was just a few months shy of turning sixty-two. His thick, blonde hair had started to grey, and his eyes were striking – piercing blue, the kind that stood out in any room. I couldn't help but notice that the color was remarkably similar to mine.

As we sat down and began to eat, I noticed Doug's hands were trembling. His whole demeanor was uneasy. He was visibly nervous, shifting in his seat, avoiding prolonged eye contact, and fidgeting with his silverware. I tried to stay calm and grounded. I didn't want to provoke him in any manner. My goal was simply to gather information. I wanted to give him a chance to speak freely, without judgment or pressure.

By this time, Joseph and I had already learned the details of Sybil's attack. It wasn't something we took lightly. We were fully aware of the possibility that the man sitting across that table might have been involved. But there was also a chance – however slim – that Doug's connection to Sybil was something entirely separate. Maybe they had met in another way. Maybe there was no violence involved. We had to remain open to every angle.

I wanted to make the meeting as non-confrontational as possible, so I framed my questions carefully. I gave him space to offer his own explanation. I suggested possibilities to make the situation less threatening – like a one-night stand or a chance meeting in a bar. I even showed him a photo of Sybil from her 20s, hoping it might trigger a memory or a moment of honesty.

Doug looked at the photo and said he didn't recognize her. He claimed he had never seen her before and had no idea who she was. He repeated that he wasn't in Houston then and that there was no way he could be involved. But something in his tone didn't sit right. He wasn't just denying. He was dodging.

Throughout our lunch, a few comments Doug made stood out to me in ways I couldn't ignore.

At one point, completely unprompted, he asked, "How is she doing? It's been so long."

I hadn't even told him Sybil was still alive. And if he truly didn't know her, why would he ask how she was doing? Why would he say "it's been so long" if he'd never seen her before?

Another moment that caught me off guard was when Doug suddenly said, "I've never been to Market Street in the East Houston area."

That was an incredibly specific statement. Too specific. I had never mentioned where Sybil lived or where the attack occurred. He had no reason to bring up that location – unless he knew something.

As we wrapped up lunch, I felt heavy. Not because I hadn't received answers, but because I felt like I had just stepped into something deeper than I anticipated. Doug was pleasant on the surface and polite enough, but the way he avoided certain questions, the things he said without realizing, and the nervous energy he carried – it all told me there was more beneath the surface.

I had one more question I wanted to ask before we ended our conversation that day. I weighed my words carefully, trying to choose the right way to bring up the topic of a DNA test. I didn't want to scare Doug off by appearing too forward or pushy; however, I knew that a DNA test would be the only way I could know for sure, without a doubt, that he was my biological father.

I took a deep breath and finally asked Doug, "Would you be willing to take a DNA test? That would prove that you are my father, or a cousin, or even an uncle."

At this point, I figured I didn't have anything to lose, and maybe I would even find some definitive answers.

Doug paused for a minute before he responded. He didn't say yes or no; he more or less dodged the question.

I left that restaurant confused, frustrated, and restless. On one hand, I had gotten what I came for. I had met Doug, looked him in the eye, and given him every chance to be honest. But I walked away with more questions than answers. It felt like he was holding something back, like he was choosing his words carefully.

I felt like Doug was playing games with me. Doug's behavior during that meeting didn't give me peace. It gave me pause. The entire interaction felt performative. Deep down, I felt there was much more to this story; I just could not put a finger on it.

What made it worse was knowing I still had no way to confirm or deny anything. I had information, yes. I had DNA links, records, timelines, and suspicion. But I didn't have closure. I had added Doug to my list of possible fathers, and now I had even more reason to keep him there.

The question now became: Was Doug a cousin? An uncle? A second cousin? The relationship wasn't yet clear. But sitting across the table from him, hearing him talk, watching his expressions – it was surreal. There were features we shared. The shape of his face. The way he smiled with only one side of his mouth. I noticed all of it.

Every step forward seemed to unlock another set of complications. But I wasn't going to stop. I had come too far for that. What I needed now was to stay the course. Keep asking questions. Keep collecting details. Keep putting the puzzle together one piece at a time.

When I reconstructed the Williams family tree and interviewed several relatives, the picture started to clear. It was no longer blurred by speculation or too many unknowns. All signs pointed to Doug. He wasn't just a potential match anymore – he became my number one suspect. It wasn't a stretch. It wasn't random. This could not be a coincidence.

I kept thinking about how everything lined up. The Y-DNA test connected me to the Williams line, and Doug was one male in that family who was in Houston at the time of the attack. His history. His criminal record. His sudden appearance in this investigation. It all pointed to him. Every new piece of evidence led me back to Doug.

After our lunch meeting, I didn't hear from him for a few days. Then, out of nowhere, he started calling. The tone of those early calls was polite and friendly. He'd ask how I was doing and talk about mundane things, but the conversations always came back to one thing – whether I'd found out anything new. It was subtle, but it felt like he was checking in to see what I knew, like he was trying to gauge how close I was to something.

I'd always answer him honestly. I wasn't trying to corner him. I didn't accuse him of anything. I never pushed him in any direction. I just kept the lines open, curious to see what he might say if I let him talk freely.

During one of our conversations, I again brought up the DNA test and told Doug I would pay for it. Again, he didn't agree; however, he did show some interest and had some questions.

"How would that work?" he asked.

I had already researched some companies that performed DNA tests in Houston and found that FamilyTreeDNA had a location within a few miles of where Doug lived. I contacted the company, and they stated that they would mail a test to Doug, and he could follow the instructions and return the kit for processing.

I paused for a moment. That really made me nervous, as I had only met Doug one time and was unsure if he would do the test correctly. Or, worse, would he have someone else take the test for him just to throw me off and try to prove to me that he was not my father?

When I explained the situation to the employee at FamilyTreeDNA, they agreed that if I paid for the DNA kit, Doug could walk in, show his valid ID, and they would ensure the test was properly administered. That way, I would know for sure that Doug was the one who took the test correctly. I was ecstatic! This was not their protocol; however, they listened to my concerns and offered to assist with a workaround.

The next time I spoke to Doug, I explained that I had already paid for the DNA test. It would be easy for him. He just needed to walk into FamilyTreeDNA and provide his ID; they would take care of everything for him.

To my surprise, Doug agreed! I was thrilled to finally have some answers!

The FamilyTreeDNA staff were so helpful; now, all I could do was wait for Doug to go in and take the test! I would finally have the answers I was looking for.

A few days later, the phone rang, and when I answered, it was FamilyTreeDNA calling. They told me that Doug had come in to take the test! Yes! I was so excited! However, my excitement quickly faded when the employee told me that Doug had a lot of questions and was very nervous. Although they had answered all his questions, Doug suddenly turned around and walked out in a state of agitation – without taking the test!

I was so disappointed! I felt I was so close, but now I was so far from verifying the truth! I felt like I had just won the lottery, only to realize that one of the numbers didn't match.

Then, something shifted.

After a few weeks of silence, Doug called me again – but this time was different. From the moment I answered, his voice was unrecognizable. It was as if I were speaking to an entirely different person. There was no politeness. No casual tone. He was angry, distressed, and erratic. The first words out of his mouth were laced with anxiety.

"This all has made me so anxious, I've started smoking again," he said. His voice trembled – not from sadness but from frustration, panic, or both. I barely had a chance to respond before he continued.

"I cannot go back to prison. I would never survive. Do you understand me? I can't." He went on, rapid-fire, not letting me get a word in, "I haven't slept in days. I haven't eaten right. I've talked to people at my church and even contacted my parole officer."

That last part caught me off guard.

"My parole officer assured me there's nothing you can do to me," Doug said, his voice rising. "The statute of limitations for rape has expired – so bring it on, buddy. Bring it on!"

He practically dared me to pursue it. It wasn't just defensive – it was aggressive. Unnerved. Full of pressure and fear.

I listened quietly as he kept talking, my heart pounding. The shift in tone – the fear and anger he had built up – said more than his actual words ever could.

What struck me most wasn't just what he said. It was the implication behind it.

Why was he talking about rape charges? Why was he so worried about the statute of limitations? Why was he panicking? If he had nothing to hide, why was he making calls to his parole officer? Why was he even thinking about prison?

At that moment, everything solidified in my mind. I was convinced.

Doug was one of the men who raped Sybil on October 30, 1978.

No, I didn't have a confession. I didn't have a paternity test signed and certified. But I had something else – context. The kind of context you can't manufacture.

I had my Y-DNA results. I had family connections. I had timelines and records that put Doug in Houston when Sybil was attacked. I had his criminal record. I had his listing on the sex offender registry. And now, I had this call – this intense, volatile outburst from a man who had, until now, been composed and polite.

I didn't want to believe it, but deep down, I did. I felt it in my body. It settled in my chest like a heavy weight I couldn't shake.

The man I had recently met for lunch – the man who looked me in the eye and denied everything – was the same man I now believed was my biological father and the man who raped my birth mother.

That realization did something to me. It cracked something open. It took away the distance I had managed to maintain through most of this journey. Up until that moment, my research had been methodical. Focused. Scientific, in a way. I was trying to build a case, find the truth, and put the puzzle together.

But this moment pulled it all into focus with a sharpness that cut deep. Suddenly, it wasn't just about piecing together a mystery. It was about facing the fact that my very existence was the result of something violent. Something non-consensual. Something traumatic.

The night after Doug's call, I couldn't sleep. And neither could Joseph. I tossed and turned, haunted by the sound of Doug's voice in my head. That rage. That panic. That raw fear.

The night terrors returned with a vengeance. I woke up screaming, drenched in sweat. I ran through the house, convinced someone was chasing me with a knife. Joseph held me until I calmed down, but nothing truly soothed me. That feeling of being unsafe, of being watched, of being followed – it all came rushing back. I had lived with it before, but now it was stronger, more vivid.

This wasn't just about fear anymore. It was about danger.

Doug's last call made something very clear – he didn't want to be exposed. He didn't want to be connected to this story. He didn't want me to ask questions or dig deeper. And that made him unpredictable.

After that call, I cut off communication entirely. I didn't text. I didn't call. I didn't return his voicemails. I had to protect myself. And I had to protect Joseph.

But it wasn't just Doug I lost contact with.

In the days and weeks that followed, Doug began reaching out to some of his family members – the same ones I had been talking to. I started noticing that people weren't returning my calls anymore. Messages went unanswered. Conversations dried up. And when I finally heard back from one cousin, he told me, "Doug told some of the family that you work for the FBI."

That was his way of isolating me and making me sound like a threat. Scare people away from helping me. And unfortunately, it worked. People stopped responding. They pulled back. I went from having connections to the Williams family to being completely shut out.

It was an isolating moment. I had just found what I truly believed to be the answer – the identity of my biological father – and suddenly, every door that had been open to me slammed shut. Not because of what I said or did, but because of what Doug feared I might do.

Even though I didn't have 100% proof, I felt the truth settle into place. I had solved the puzzle. I had traced my roots. I had followed the timeline. And every thread led back to Douglas Lamar Williams.

My focus narrowed. No more broad searches. No more casting a wide net. From then on, it was about one man. Doug.

I didn't know if I would ever be able to prove it beyond a shadow of a doubt. But I knew what I felt. I knew what I had seen in his eyes. I knew what he had said on that call. And I knew what my gut was telling me – loud and clear.

All signs pointed to Doug.

Chapter 5: A Darker Pattern Emerges

After that final phone call, I made a firm decision – no more communication with Doug. I didn't need any more of his cryptic answers or hostile tones. The way his voice cracked, the panic, the anger, the bizarre admission about the statute of limitations for rape – it was all too much. I knew he was on the sex offender registry. I already knew about his criminal past. I was convinced he was one of the three men who had raped and nearly killed my birth mother.

But what I didn't know was what else he was capable of. And I didn't know what he might do next, especially now that he realized someone was digging into his past. That uncertainty – paired with the raw terror in his voice when he talked about not going back to prison – was enough to push me into silence.

Not out of weakness. Out of instinct.

I didn't trust him and couldn't predict what he'd do if he thought I threatened his freedom. He seemed desperate. Cornered. Maybe even volatile. And in that space, my night terrors came back stronger than ever. The same old patterns – waking up drenched in sweat, running through the house in the dark, yelling out in fear, waking Joseph from sleep with my screams. It felt like my subconscious had its own alarm system, triggered by the warning signs Doug had given me loud and clear.

Cutting off communication meant I lost access to any potential insight into the Williams family. Doug also made sure of that. By telling some of his relatives that I was an FBI agent, he effectively shut down any remaining avenues I had on that side. People stopped returning my calls. A few blocked me outright. It was like someone flipped a switch – radio silence.

But that didn't mean I was done.

If I couldn't talk to Doug, then fine. I'd talk to the paper trail instead. Police reports. Arrest records. Probation records. Court documents. If it were in the public records, I was going to find it. I dove deep into online databases, city archives, and even old newspaper clippings. I dug through family trees, old address books, and city directories. I started building timelines, tracking patterns, and matching locations to dates. It became almost methodical – something I could control in the middle of a situation that felt impossible to navigate emotionally.

That's when I found it.

Buried in a set of public records from late 1978 – just two months after the night my mother had been attacked – I came across an arrest report that immediately stopped me in my tracks. It involved Doug.

The details in the report weren't vague or speculative. They were explicit. Violent. Disturbing. I read through the narrative in disbelief. Two months after the night Sybil was left for dead, Doug had been accused of doing something horrifyingly similar again – this time in a completely different part of town.

It shook me.

It wasn't just a one-time act of violence anymore. It was a pattern. A dark, dangerous pattern. And it was documented. This wasn't something whispered about or rumored. It was official. It had happened. And the man I had sat across from at lunch – the man who had nervously gripped the edge of the table, who had claimed he didn't know Sybil, who had asked me in a half-slip, "How is she doing?" – was the same man being accused of a similar sexual assault crime just weeks after the attack on my birth mother, Sybil.

Doug hadn't just been a possibility. He had a documented history of violent behavior that matched the very crime that changed my mother's life – and created mine.

I couldn't stop thinking about that police report. The pattern was there now – etched in the public record. And if there was one, there could be others.

I stayed up for days, running names, cross-checking dates, and digging through everything I could find tied to Doug – no matter how far removed. That's how I stumbled across this police report. Names I didn't recognize at first, but that would soon become another piece of this expanding puzzle: Leroy Hubert Giese, also known as "Buddy" and his wife, Eugenia Erline "Learlene" Gilbert.

The report was graphic.

On December 16, 1978, Buddy and Learlene left their condo around 10:00 a.m. They had planned to go to Clute, Texas, to pick up a few items from Tom's Pawn Shop. It should've been a simple, ordinary errand, but life throws the unexpected in our paths. Buddy spotted a man standing outside their condo who appeared to be looking for a ride. Something about him must have caught Buddy's attention because he offered him a lift.

The man introduced himself as Doug. He said he had just spent three days in jail and was released that morning. There was no mention of what he'd been in for, no details about the past, or any reason for his arrest. But something about the way he said it – offhand, almost dismissive – raised a red flag for me as I pored over the police reports.

After picking up Doug, they stopped by the Freeport Post Office and then went to a local bank. Doug was with them, just another man in their company all the while, but his presence seemed to weigh heavily on the day. The trio made their way to a lounge, where they drank a few beers. I couldn't shake the oddity of it all.

Why were Buddy and Learlene spending time with a man who had just been released from jail?

Allegedly, they didn't know him.

What was it about Doug that made them invite him along?

By the time the sun began to set, they had bounced from one bar to another, drinking away the hours. The night wore on. They had no agenda or pressing reason to be out together, but they still carried on. It felt as if they were merely killing time, moving from one distraction to the next, until they finally made their way to the pawn shop.

The day had been a blur of stops, drinks, and chatter – something to pass the time, something to dull whatever heaviness they were all carrying. The pawn shop was the last place they visited, but by 11:00 p.m., they were back at their condo, a place that should've been quiet and filled with the remnants of the day's aimlessness.

Learlene, tired and perhaps ready to just call it a night, fixed Doug a place to sleep on the couch. It seemed like an innocent enough gesture – after all, they had spent the whole day together. Yet, as the night stretched, it became clear that whatever had been simmering beneath the surface for hours was finally coming to a boil.

After Learlene prepared the place on the couch for Doug to sleep, she went into the bathroom to take a shower. A few minutes later, the door opened, and there stood Doug. Just staring at Learlene, naked. Buddy tried to shove her out of the way and told her to put some clothes on. Doug then hit Buddy. When Learlene tried to get between them, Doug knocked her down.

The noise from the altercation was loud enough to draw the attention of an upstairs neighbor, who came down to investigate. It wasn't clear how much of the fight they witnessed, but Learlene's version of events painted a specific picture. According to her, she told the neighbor that Buddy had picked up a hitchhiker who was now "beating them up." Doug, the man they had spent the entire day with, had become the aggressor. And in an instant, the situation flipped. No longer was Doug just a stranger they'd picked up, a man they had shared drinks with and invited into their home. He was now a threat – a danger.

The fight seemed to have reached a peak quickly. When the neighbor called the Sheriff's Department, Doug left immediately. There were no signs of bloodshed or physical violence that followed him out the door, but the tension lingered. The encounter with Doug was over, but something about the entire episode didn't sit right.

What struck me as particularly odd was the entire sequence of events that had led up to this moment.

Why, out of all the people Buddy and Learlene could have met on that day, did they pick up a man like Doug?

They spent thirteen hours with him, driving around, drinking together, and then, without hesitation, they offered him a bed on their couch for the night. It didn't make sense.

Why let a stranger into their home?

There was something about this interaction that didn't add up.

What about Doug made them so willing to open their doors to him?

Was it his charm, his apparent normalcy despite his jail stint?

Or was there something darker at play here?

I couldn't shake the feeling that this wasn't just a random encounter – it was a thread that could unravel everything I thought I knew.

Then, Learlene framed the whole situation when she spoke to the neighbor. She described Doug as if he was the problem, as if he had turned on them without warning.

But was that the truth, or was it a convenient narrative to explain what had gone wrong that night?

What if the story wasn't as simple as she made it sound?

Less than a week later, on Friday, December 22, 1978, Buddy and Learlene went to bed around 9:30 p.m. The apartment was quiet, the kind of stillness that only settles in when everyone's winding down for the night. But that peace didn't last long. Thirty minutes later, at exactly 10:00 p.m., a knock at the door cut through the silence, snapping Learlene out of her sleep.

Startled, she shook Buddy awake. Without a word, he slipped on his pants, and Learlene – still in her nightgown – draped Buddy's robe over her shoulders, a half-hearted attempt at covering up the confusion of being woken from a deep sleep. But whatever had roused Doug from whatever he was doing that night, it was clear he wasn't interested in subtlety.

When Buddy opened the door, Doug didn't wait for an invitation. He barged in, his presence as aggressive as it was unexpected. Without any pleasantries, he demanded to know if they had anything to drink. Learlene, still shaken, calmly told him they didn't.

But Doug wasn't deterred. He asked Buddy if he wanted to go out and get something to drink, but Buddy refused. It was a simple exchange, nothing out of the ordinary, except that it wasn't. Doug's sudden appearance felt more like a demand than a visit. His frantic and unpredictable energy settled like a heavy cloud in the room.

Then, out of nowhere, Doug made a shocking claim. He told Buddy that he owed him money. The accusation hung in the air, thick with hostility. As I read through the reports, I couldn't help but wonder about Doug's motives. What exactly was he trying to accomplish? Was this just another layer of the chaos he was sowing, or was there something deeper at play?

Doug's behavior became more violent when he noticed Buddy's money clip. Doug reached into Buddy's pocket without hesitation, pulling out the clip and a set of car keys. He flipped through the bills quickly, his eyes scanning them before muttering that it wasn't enough. He stalked over to the bedroom and returned with Buddy's gun a few moments later – a Colt .38 Special revolver, the kind with a 6-inch barrel, blue steel, and a plastic grip.

Buddy had shown Doug the gun a few days earlier, but now, it was a tool of intimidation, a weapon in Doug's hands.

Doug stepped into the living room with the gun raised. He shoved Buddy down onto the couch, and before Buddy could react, Doug held the barrel of the revolver inches from his head.

"I ought to kill you," Doug told Buddy.

The cold metal against Buddy's skin was a stark reminder of how quickly the situation had escalated. Doug wasn't just angry; he was enraged, using the gun as a means to control, to terrorize. His voice was low and threatening, and he ordered Buddy and Learlene to take off their clothes.

What followed was a nightmare. Doug, fueled by whatever twisted impulses drove him, crossed every boundary. The graphic details of what happened next are beyond words. It was a violation of the most personal kind, an act of cruelty that left Buddy and Learlene broken in ways I can't even begin to describe. Doug was the perpetrator of that violence, and their suffering at his hands was something I had never imagined encountering in any report, any statement, any piece of testimony.

But the chaos didn't end there.

Learlene, trying to maintain some semblance of control over the situation, asked Doug if she could get dressed. The request, simple as it seemed, was a small shred of normalcy amidst the madness. After a brief pause, Doug told her she could go ahead. She made her way into the bedroom to change, but even that act felt meaningless in the face of everything that had transpired.

Doug finally let Buddy put his clothes on.

"Doug," Buddy asked, "give me back my car keys."

Doug refused and instead demanded, "Give me the bill of sale for the car."

Somehow, Buddy convinced Doug that he did not know where the papers were.

Doug then instructed Buddy to write a note stating that he was giving the gun to Doug. When Doug read the note, he became angry, tore the note up, and dictated another note for Buddy to write.

Once Learlene returned, Doug's focus shifted again. He motioned for her to sit down. However, his eyes never left Buddy, and he took him by the arm and led him into the bedroom. It felt like an eternity passed in the quiet that followed, a suffocating weight pressing down on Learlene in the living room as she waited, helpless.

Doug then threatened Buddy by saying, "I could kill you, throw you in the canal, and get away with it."

"You just get Learlene to promise not to leave the house," Doug told Buddy, "and I will take you somewhere, give you back the car, gun, and money."

When Doug and Buddy finally emerged from the bedroom, Buddy looked different. Gone was the man who had been sitting at the kitchen table just hours before, the man who had tried to resist Doug's threats, even with the gun pointed at him. Now, Buddy's voice was low, strained, as he spoke to Learlene.

He told her, "If you don't call the police, Doug will take me somewhere, so he will give back the car, gun, and the money."

Learlene's face was a mixture of confusion and disbelief.

"How long am I supposed to sit and wait?" she asked, her voice shaking, but Doug's response was chilling.

"Two hours," he said coldly, "and if you leave the apartment, Buddy is dead. I will knock him in the head and throw him in the canal."

The words hung in the air, each one carrying the weight of something far more sinister than I could fully comprehend. And then, just like that, Doug and Buddy left the apartment, the door slamming shut behind them. Learlene was left in the silence, trembling, every minute stretching into what felt like hours.

Once outside, Doug unlocked Buddy's 1977 Toyota Land Cruiser. Doug got in the driver's seat and made Buddy sit in the passenger seat. After driving across the Surfside Bridge, Doug parked the car under the bridge.

"I ought to kill you," Doug said.

Buddy, terrified, never said a word.

Doug and Buddy sat there for about ten minutes, watching the house to ensure Learlene had not called the police.

"I will give you the gun and money back," Doug told Buddy. "Drive home, wait thirty minutes, and then meet me at Beach Bait and Tackle."

Doug made Buddy look at his watch. It was now 12:08 a.m., the morning of December 23rd.

Buddy sat and watched Doug as he walked toward Beach Bait and Tackle before driving home.

Doug and Buddy had been gone for about an hour. When Learlene saw Buddy walk in the door, his face was drawn, his expression hard to read, but something in his eyes spoke volumes of the tension, the fear, the confusion.

"I am supposed to meet Doug at Beach Bait and Tackle in 30 minutes," Buddy said. "Doug agreed to give back the money and the gun."

It was clear that Buddy was just as trapped in this mess as Learlene was. The gun, the threat, and the fear that had plagued them both had left their mark, and now, they had no choice but to follow through. They left the condo, heading toward Beach Bait and Tackle as planned. But when they arrived, there was no sign of Doug. No gun. No money.

But as they drove down the road, Learlene caught sight of a police car in the distance. Buddy's instincts kicked in, and he told Learlene to pull over. With urgency, he got out of the car and approached the officer. It was almost like a desperate plea for help, an attempt to make sense of the chaos that had taken over their lives.

Buddy wasted no time. He went straight to the officer, his words coming out quickly, laced with a mix of anger and fear.

"A white male, known only to me as 'Doug' raped my wife and robbed me of $80.00 in cash and a .38 special revolver," he said. "I last saw him under the Surfside Bridge."

The words were hard to hear, harder still to understand, but they were the truth. The raw, unvarnished truth that had been buried in their home just hours before.

Learlene stood by, her voice shaky but determined as she spoke to the officer.

"I did not want to have any kind of sex with Doug," she said, her words rushed but clear, "but I feared for my life if I didn't do what he said."

The officer nodded, making notes as Learlene's statement settled into the tense air of the night. It wasn't long before the police set off to find Doug. They scoured the area, looking for anyone matching the description Buddy had given. Hours passed, the air thick with the weight of anticipation. Finally, the officers found a man fitting Doug's description perfectly. They brought him in, and Buddy was called to identify him.

Buddy stood before the suspect at the station, his eyes narrowed, studying every feature. He knew the man, but seeing Doug now, after everything that had happened, felt surreal. The officer stood by, watching as Buddy confirmed the man in front of him was, without a doubt, Doug. His voice was firm when he said it, but there was no mistaking the emotion behind his words – the recognition of a man who had just destroyed so much.

Doug didn't show any remorse. He remained stone-faced, his expression unreadable. As the officers began to search Doug, they found what they were looking for. In his front pocket, tucked away in a place that should have been private, was the .38 special revolver. The very gun he had used to terrorize Buddy and Learlene. Along with it was $85.00 in cash and a money clip, as if he had been collecting his "payoff" from whatever scheme he was running. It was clear now that Doug wasn't just some random criminal who had crossed their path. This was a man with a purpose and a ruthless disregard for human decency.

Doug was arrested on the spot, and the officers transported him to the Brazoria County Jail. He was charged with Aggravated Rape, Unlawfully Carrying a Weapon, and Aggravated Robbery. The bond was set at $51,000. A hefty sum, but not nearly enough to erase the trauma he had caused. It was just a number on a piece of paper, a technicality amid the devastation he had left behind.

When they attempted to interview Doug, he immediately clammed up.

"My attorney is Percy Foreman," he stated with cold indifference, "and I will not give an interview without my attorney present."

The statement was almost formal, as if he had rehearsed it a hundred times before. Doug knew his rights, but he also knew that the evidence against him was damning. It didn't matter how much legal maneuvering he did – it wouldn't change what had happened that night.

Doug eventually accepted a plea bargain for felony robbery. He served about six years in prison, a far cry from the full extent of the damage he had caused. There were no details on what had transpired during those six years, but for Buddy and Learlene, the time spent in the legal system felt like nothing more than a distraction from the emotional and psychological toll they would continue to face.

There were still a lot of unanswered questions.

Was there something deeper at play here?

Had Buddy and Doug known each other before that night?

Could their involvement have gone beyond mere chance, perhaps involving some "shady" dealings neither Buddy nor Learlene fully understood?

Maybe Buddy and Doug were involved on some deeper level, and Learlene was in the dark.

These were questions that didn't have clear answers, and even as the case went to trial, they lingered in the background like ghosts. Could the true nature of Doug's relationship with Buddy have been hidden, leaving Learlene to navigate a world of pain and confusion she had never fully anticipated?

But one revelation still shocked me to the core, something that tied everything together in a way I couldn't have predicted. It wasn't just Doug's criminal history or the twisted chain of events surrounding Buddy and Learlene. It was a shocking connection – a victim that turned out to be my own mother-in-law's cousin. An incredible coincidence that suddenly made everything feel far more personal.

In early 2012, I became completely consumed by my research. I was obsessed, unable to let go of the case that had twisted deeply into my life. I spent countless sleepless nights combing through reports, searching for any information that might unlock the mystery. It was like an itch I couldn't scratch. One night, around 1:00 a.m., Joseph was fast asleep beside me, and I was struggling with insomnia. My brain wouldn't shut off. I was diving deeper and deeper into Learlene's story, and as the hours ticked by, I decided to search her name on Ancestry.com.

What I found that night took me by complete surprise. Eugenia Erline "Learlene" Gilbert Giese was in my husband's family tree! The connection was undeniable – there, among cousins, was a name I had researched for months. It was the kind of revelation that stopped me in my tracks. I had spent so much time trying to understand the nature of Doug's crimes, but this discovery – this link to my husband's family – was a surprise connection I hadn't anticipated.

Joseph was sound asleep, breathing steadily beside me, completely unaware of what I had found. I knew he had to be up early for work in the morning, and the last thing I wanted to do was wake him. But I couldn't keep this to myself. My mind was racing. I needed to tell anyone who might understand just how big this discovery was.

There was only one person who came to mind: Callie.

She had given me the DNA kit as a Christmas gift back in 2009, and it had turned out to be the most life-altering gift I'd ever received. From the moment I began unraveling the truth about my biological family, that little kit had become the thread pulling everything together. And now, it had led me to this – the connection between my story, my past, and someone in Callie's own family. If anyone would appreciate the gravity of what I'd just uncovered, it was her.

So, without hesitation, I picked up the phone and dialed. It was late – well after 1:00 a.m. – but I knew Callie. She was a night owl through and through. Thankfully, she answered after just a few rings.

"Hello?" she said, her voice alert despite the hour.

"Callie," I blurted, trying to keep my voice steady, "do you know a Eugenia Learlene Gilbert Giese?"

There was a pause, and then she responded with absolute certainty, "Yes! That's my dad's first cousin!"

I sat there frozen for a second, stunned by the confirmation.

"You're sure?" I asked.

"Absolutely," she said. "I remember her. Her name was Erline, but people called her Learlene. Why?"

I could hardly believe what I was hearing. My head spun. The ironies. The coincidences.

Joseph. What were the odds of meeting him in Houston? In a city where millions of people aimlessly and meticulously go about their lives daily… and I meet someone from the same religious background with the same deep love for family.

Callie. Joseph' mother. Meeting her in 2009. The year she gave me the DNA kit that had started all of this – my search for identity, truth, and connection.

Who could have imagined that more than 30 years before I ever met Callie, Douglas Lamar Williams – my biological father – had raped one of her relatives at gunpoint? Right in front of Learlene's husband, Leroy "Buddy" Giese.

It was almost too much to wrap my mind around. There had been no reason to ever suspect a connection like this.

I was still reeling from the connection between Learlene and Callie when a new wave of questions flooded my mind.

If Doug had done this to Learlene – someone connected to my inner circle without me even knowing – what else had he done? Had there been other victims?

More assaults?

Arrests that were never spoken of again?

I couldn't shake the thought that maybe these two cases – my mother, Sybil, and now Learlene – weren't isolated incidents. Maybe they were just the tip of something much deeper.

So, I went back into the reports and dug further. I started cross-referencing dates, arrest records, and crime logs. I looked into every corner of Doug's past I could get my hands on. I was obsessive, but I couldn't help it. I had to know. A pattern was starting to take shape, even if it was still blurry around the edges.

The only phrase that kept echoing in my head was, "Truth is stranger than fiction." Nothing about this journey had followed any kind of logic I could have predicted. Whenever I thought I'd found the edge of the story, something else pushed the line further out.

The deeper I went, the harder it became to pull myself away. The connection to Learlene had opened a door I didn't even know existed, and behind it were more questions than answers. It was like falling down a rabbit hole. Only this one was filled with arrest records, newspaper clippings, court documents, and other people's pain fragments.

You can imagine my shock when I read the police reports and court transcripts surrounding this event. My stomach churned as I connected the dots between this case and my lingering questions about my own family's history. It was as though the universe had placed this information in front of me for a reason – perhaps a chance to uncover something hidden for years.

I continued to search each of the victims and their families to see if there were any similarities to my mother's assault, which had happened only two months earlier. The more I dug into the details, the more my mind raced. I meticulously analyzed police reports and records, posing questions to myself.

Could there be something in the patterns?

Were these victims connected in a way that would explain Doug's strange behavior, his targeting of certain individuals?

The connection was hard to deny. It felt like the answer was slipping through my fingers, just beyond reach. But one question stood out, and it haunted me more than any other: *What led Doug to target Sybil, my birth mom, specifically?*

Why her? Out of all the people in the world, why had Doug chosen Sybil as his victim?

It didn't make sense to me at first. She wasn't just another victim in a string of crimes. There had to be a reason for it – something more than a random selection.

I even took a close look at the investigators who processed the crime scenes, the victims, and the witnesses. I dug into their backgrounds, trying to find something that might explain why Doug had been able to slip through the cracks. I constructed family trees for the victims, hoping to find some link or common thread explaining their selection of Sybil. Maybe, just maybe, this approach would provide valuable insights into his motives – into what made him target her, in particular.

Finding that report was huge. It wasn't just another document – it was detailed, specific, undeniable. For the first time, I had proof that Doug wasn't only capable of what Sybil had endured; he had already been arrested for the same kind of crime. And he hadn't been in prison at the time of Sybil's attack. But even with that breakthrough, I still had more questions than answers. Why the Gieses? Was it random, an act of convenience? Or did Doug have a method, some way of selecting his victims that wasn't visible at first glance? If I could understand that, maybe I could understand something even harder – how and why he had picked my mother.

The deeper the investigation went, the clearer it became: Doug didn't just "happen upon" people. There was something in the way he chose – something in the pattern I hadn't uncovered yet.

Nothing was ever labeled as the work of a serial predator, but I was starting to see it. I knew the language now. I had read enough about sexual assault offenders to recognize the signatures. Threats. Weapons. Control. Violence. Disregard for consent. He didn't just hurt women – he targeted them, manipulated them, and took what he wanted.

Looking back, it's almost unbelievable that so much of this had gone unnoticed for so long. Or maybe it hadn't gone unnoticed – maybe people had just chosen not to see it. But once I started seeing the signs, I couldn't unsee them.

I kept working through every detail I could get my hands on. I started calling courthouses, requesting documents, and checking for police reports under different variations of his name. Doug, Douglas, Lamar, D.L. Williams. I learned you must be creative when looking into someone's past. People like him didn't always leave a clean paper trail. They left victims. And those victims, even if they didn't press charges, had stories. I began looking into those, too.

I created spreadsheets. I color-coded incidents based on the level of violence. I flagged known aliases. I kept track of dates that overlapped with my own life, trying to understand how close I had unknowingly been to this man's crimes. Sometimes, the reality of it made me sick. Other times, it made me more determined. I didn't know exactly what I hoped to find – confirmation, maybe. A full picture. The truth.

And what I kept finding pointed to one thing: Doug wasn't just a bad man. He was a sexual predator. A serial one.

This wasn't something I ever expected to learn about the man whose DNA I carried. But I couldn't look away now. The facts were stacking up. The attacks weren't isolated. The pattern was there, even if no one had ever called it what it was.

Without warning, the facts, attacks, and patterns were about to take a sharp, deadly twist.

Chapter 6: Deadly Coincidences

The more I turned my attention to Buddy and Learlene, the stranger the story became. Leroy "Buddy" Hubert Giese was born in 1926 and was more than two decades older than Doug.

Buddy worked as a chemist at Dow Chemical and had a personal life that read more like a maze than a timeline. He cycled through six marriages to four women. Two of those women reappeared again and again. It was an on-again, off-again pattern that felt chaotic even by 1970s standards.

That's where my first real puzzle appeared. Police reports from December 1978 list Buddy and Learlene as husband and wife. But the marriage records told a different story.

Buddy and Learlene Giese were *not* married!

I rechecked the marriage and divorce dates. I carefully reread the police reports documenting Doug's attack on them in December 1978. It was there. It was clearly stated. Buddy and Learlene referred to each other multiple times as husband and wife. I checked the marriage and divorce dates again and built a timeline. What was going on?

Buddy and Learlene were first married on May 8, 1947, and divorced on May 9, 1970. The next part made me stop and double-check the records. Just sixteen days after their divorce was final, on May 25, 1970, they married again. Their second attempt lasted almost five years, ending in divorce on April 7, 1975.

But wait. By every official record I could find, Buddy and Learlene had been divorced for more than three years when Doug attacked them in December 1978.

What was going on?

The timeline kept turning up more twists. Six months after his second divorce from Learlene, Buddy married Martha Jane Grant on October 16, 1975.

Learlene also moved on. She remarried. This time to James Arthur Sisk on December 19, 1977. She was just shy of 49. James was nearly 30 years older than her.

I stopped again. Not only was Learlene divorced from Buddy when Doug attacked them, she was legally married to another man, James Sisk – and for only one year.

It was a tangled web, but it wasn't until I started mapping it out that I realized just how strange and volatile things were in 1978.

That year seemed to pull everyone back into each other's orbit.

I turned my focus to Buddy's current wife, Martha Jane Grant Giese. Who was she? I wanted to know more of her story, but the plot kept taking more turns.

That's when I discovered that Buddy's wife, Martha, had been arrested and was awaiting trial for murder.

Murder?

Yes, murder.

The murder of 35-year-old Melvin Douglas Schott.

Who was Melvin? And how did he connect to this story?

Melvin's family provided a disturbing narrative of how the events unfolded. Early in 1978, Buddy was involved in an accident. He struck Melvin with his car. Melvin survived, but the injuries were severe. Melvin was confined to a wheelchair. The family later told me they believed Melvin had filed a civil lawsuit against Buddy for damages related to the accident. The timing was important because it would set off a deadly chain of events that no one could've scripted.

By April 17, 1978, Buddy and Martha divorced. But that break didn't last long either. Just four months later, they remarried on August 23, 1978. That detail eerily reminded me of how Buddy and Learlene had divorced and quickly remarried in 1970. People don't usually leap in and out of marriages that quickly unless something deep and unresolved is boiling under the surface.

Then came October.

On Saturday, October 7, 1978, Melvin Schott met Buddy and Martha at a residence in Texas City. Something escalated. According to the newspaper, an argument began around 7:45 p.m. and quickly turned into a physical altercation. At some point during the confrontation, Martha grabbed a .22-caliber rifle and shot Melvin in the back.

It wasn't a warning shot. Melvin was rushed to Memorial Hospital in Galveston and died during surgery less than an hour later.

Martha was arrested. She was charged with murder and placed in jail on a $10,000 bond.

At this point, I was reading these reports in stunned silence. Doug was already at the center of one traumatic event after another in my life, but now here was a completely separate situation – another family, another circle of violence – and it was still tied to him.

The deeper I looked into it, the weirder it got.

Within weeks after the shooting, in the early hours of Thursday, November 23, 1978, Martha was involved in another incident – this time, a car accident. Around 1:00 a.m., Thanksgiving morning, she was pulling out of a private driveway on Main Street in Houston when she was struck by another vehicle. She was pronounced dead less than an hour later at Ben Taub General Hospital.

The autopsy reported that her cause of death was a ruptured spleen caused by the impact. But what really stood out was that her blood alcohol content was 0.271 – more than double the legal limit in Texas at that time.

Officially, it was ruled a fatal accident. However, the stories people shared didn't line up neatly.

I spoke with a few people who had known Martha – some family members and a few locals who had pieced together details over the years. No one could agree on what happened that night. Some said it was a high-speed chase. Others hinted at suicide. A few whispered foul play – that someone wanted her gone before the trial. The speculation only made the reality more unsettling. No one seemed to know for sure what Martha was doing that night or who might've wanted her gone.

I researched every detail. That's when I found one more detail that unsettled me further. The officer who responded to Martha's fatal accident wasn't just any patrolman. He was a Houston officer who, not long before, had been accused of homicide himself. Not once but twice. Though both were ultimately ruled "justifiable homicide," the cases had always carried a cloud of suspicion. For him to be the one standing over Martha's body in the early hours of Thanksgiving morning felt less like a coincidence and more like another thread in a web I still couldn't see in full.

The timeline kept looming in my research. Dates that wouldn't match neatly but then spiral into new revelations. I had already verified that Buddy and Learlene had been married and divorced twice for more than three years when they were attacked by Doug in December 1978. Vital Statistics records revealed that Learlene was also married to another man, James Sisk. Now, the realization hit me that Buddy himself stood shrouded in grief – his own wife, Martha had been recently laid to rest.

The uncanny 1978 timeline hit me in the face.

Early in 1978, Buddy injured Melven Schott.

On April 17, Buddy and Martha divorced.

On August 23, Buddy and Martha remarried.

On October 7, Martha allegedly shot and killed Melvin.

On October 30, Doug and three other men raped and assaulted Sybil.

On November 23, Martha was killed.

On December 16, only three weeks later, Buddy and Learlene picked up Doug as an alleged hitchhiker. That encounter ended in an altercation.

On December 23, 1978, exactly one month after Martha had passed, Doug brutally assaulted Buddy and Learlene at gunpoint.

Even stranger: within days of Martha's death, Learlene had already moved back in with Buddy. The same Learlene had been married twice and divorced from Buddy. The same Learlene who was still legally married to James Sisk.

Learlene didn't move in with Buddy to just any residence or random address. She moved back to the same home Buddy and Martha had shared at 26 Sailfish Drive in Freeport, Texas. The Bridge Harbor Yacht Club condominium facing the Intercoastal Waterway was still in Buddy and Martha's names.

She didn't wait for any respectful amount of time. There was no public mourning. No distance. She just... moved back in like none of it had ever happened. It didn't look like a coincidence. It looked like momentum.

I sat with all of this. The names, the dates, the tangled marriages, the violence, the accusations, the deaths. I wasn't sure what it all meant, but I knew this wasn't just a series of isolated family squabbles gone sideways. Something darker lived at the core of this story. Something that didn't fit neatly into timelines or court documents.

There was something about this interaction that didn't add up.

I talked to Melvin's family, neighbors, and people who remembered fragments of those months. The stories were messy and sometimes contradictory, but a pattern emerged: accidents, lawsuits, sudden remarriages, a murder charge, a suspicious death, and then Doug standing in the middle of it all, demanding money. Folks I spoke with speculated – quietly, urgently – about motives and coverups.

It struck me as more than mere chance that Martha had died while she was awaiting trial for murder. Some believed Buddy had pulled the trigger and fired the shot that had killed Melvin, and Martha had taken the blame. There was speculation that Martha, a woman, would receive a lighter sentence than Buddy. And Buddy didn't want to lose his job as a chemist at Dow Chemical. Others wondered if Martha's death had been staged to look accidental.

And Doug? The police report says he demanded money Buddy owed him. Why would Buddy owe Doug anything? Had Doug been involved in something that created that debt? Or was he simply someone whose path crossed a family already unspooling?

I couldn't answer those questions with the records alone. Dates and documents map what happened, but they don't explain why people made the choices they did. They don't explain who wanted whom, or what price anyone was willing to pay.

So I left the files on the table and stared at the gaps between them. Who shot Melvin? If it wasn't Martha, why did she take the fall? Was Martha's death an accident, suicide, or something darker? Why did Learlene come back so fast, and why was Doug demanding money the same month these deaths and arrests were happening?

Too many deaths, too many divorces, too many coincidences – all circling the same names. At some point, you have to wonder if coincidence was ever part of the story at all.

Chapter 7: Digging into the Past

All I could do was keep going. Keep digging. At first, it felt like a personal search – trying to stitch together fragments of my own history – but the deeper I went, the more it took on the shape of an investigation. Each discovery wasn't just another fact; it was a clue, a pivot, a new direction that reframed everything I thought I knew.

It was less about connecting to the past and more about exposing it.

Stories began to emerge. Doug had an obvious, blatant disregard for law and order.

Arrest records began to narrate a story. They began with what might look, on the surface, like minor infractions.

Doug had multiple arrests for driving under the influence. Alone, that might not have raised eyebrows – people get DUIs, some more than once. But in the context of his life, they mattered. They revealed recklessness, disregard for safety, and a willingness to gamble with the lives of strangers on the road. It told me he lived without boundaries, that the rules which protected others meant little to him.

For the investigation, these early arrests mattered because they established a baseline: Doug was not someone living quietly, unnoticed. He was already in the system. His name was in the files. And yet, despite that visibility, he wasn't being stopped.

Then came the thefts. Again, not rare crimes. But they shifted the profile. Thefts revealed opportunism. He didn't just take risks for thrills; he took what wasn't his, whenever it suited him. He didn't respect property, didn't respect limits. The lesson for me was clear: Doug wasn't driven by desperation. He was driven by entitlement. That was a critical distinction, because entitlement is often a precursor to escalation. If you believe the rules don't apply to you, you will eventually test how far you can push that belief.

And Doug did.

The impersonation of a police officer was the first moment the investigation snapped into sharper focus. This wasn't recklessness anymore. It was manipulation. Control. Pretending to be law enforcement wasn't about petty theft or convenience; it was about power. It told me Doug wasn't content with simply breaking rules – he wanted to wield authority, to bend others to his will. That was a chilling realization.

The stabbing of his brother-in-law reinforced it further. Violence wasn't reserved for strangers. It lived inside his own home, inside his relationships. For the investigation, that mattered deeply. It meant Doug's violence wasn't about circumstance – it was about nature. It was part of who he was. If he could turn a knife on family, then what chance did anyone else have?

By this point, I could see the slope clearly. Doug's crimes were escalating. The files weren't random dots on a map; they were a timeline, pointing steadily toward greater violence. The charges and incidents accumulated as if I were watching snow turn from a dusting to a covering on the lawn.

Then, I found it. A discovery that changed everything.

March 13, 1974. Doug was 23 years old. A third documented sexual assault.

Up until then, there was still room – however slim – for me to imagine that Sybil's attack, or the assault on Buddy and Learlene Giese, had been isolated moments of rage. Awful, yes. But not necessarily proof of a larger predatory life. This case erased that possibility.

This attack confirmed what I had already started to see – this wasn't a one-time thing. There weren't even two isolated attacks. It was clear now that Doug had been committing violent crimes for years.

The report was blunt. It was spelled out: Doug raped a minor child under the age of 17. It wasn't vague, it wasn't softened. It read, "intentionally and knowingly, by force and threats."

There was no question about the nature of the crime. It was brutal and deliberate.

I sat with that for a minute. This wasn't just bad behavior or a mistake. For me, for the investigation, this was the hinge. This was when everything tilted.

Doug wasn't just reckless, violent, or entitled. His behavior was predatory. He had targeted a child. He had made a deliberate choice to exploit vulnerability in the most brutal way possible.

The fact that it happened four and a half years before my mother's assault meant something, too. It established a timeline. It showed that by the time he hurt Sybil, he was not a young man who made a single mistake. He was already a seasoned predator.

But what shocked me most was not the crime. It was what came after.

I quickly realized that the outcome didn't match the severity of the crime. The charge began as rape, a serious felony. His bail was set at $20,000 – a steep amount in 1974, showing that the court recognized the gravity of what he'd done. But by the time the case was resolved, the charge had been reduced to "indecency with a child," a Class A misdemeanor. Doug served one year in county jail, with four months shaved off for time served.

This was the moment the investigation shifted again. It wasn't just about Doug anymore. It was about the system.

It didn't make sense. How a man who had raped a child to walk away with a minor conviction and a short stint in county jail? I couldn't understand it. Was it an aggressive defense attorney who found a loophole? A prosecutor who decided the case wasn't strong enough to win at trial? Maybe the victim had been pressured not to testify. Or maybe people just didn't want to deal with the full weight of the case.

The lesson was sobering: Doug had been caught, identified, and named for what he was. And then the system let him go.

That outcome told me several things. First, I could no longer assume that the legal record reflected the full truth. If a documented rape could be massaged into a misdemeanor, then what about the cases that never even reached court? Second, it showed me that Doug had protection – because these kinds of deals don't happen by accident. Someone had argued it down. Someone had pulled strings. Someone had ensured he walked away with barely a scar.

Whatever the reason, Doug had gotten a deal that he never should have gotten.

Seeing how easily he slipped through the cracks explained a lot. If he faced real consequences back in 1974, maybe he wouldn't have been free to attack others later. But instead, he was given another chance to reenter society with barely a mark against him.

I couldn't stop thinking about the girl he hurt in 1974. I wondered what her life had been like afterward. Was she ever able to heal? Did she ever know that her attacker went on to hurt more women? I felt connected to her in a way. Both of us had our lives disrupted by the same man.

This discovery made everything about my search more urgent. I wasn't just uncovering my father's hidden past. I was exposing real damage, real lives that had been affected.

And there was no telling how many other victims there might have been.

Piece by piece, the real story was coming together. Doug's crimes weren't isolated incidents. They were part of a long, disturbing pattern. And thanks to the leniency he received early on, he had been free to continue hurting people.

Seeing it laid out in front of me in black and white made everything real in a way that words alone couldn't. It wasn't just family rumors. It wasn't just vague memories or guesses. It was documented. It had happened. And no one had done nearly enough to stop it.

The deeper I dug, the more determined I became. There was no choice but to keep going and uncover every piece of the truth I could find. I needed to know the full extent of what Doug had done. And more than that, I needed it out in the open – no more secrets, no more hiding.

It didn't take long before another piece of the puzzle came into focus. As I kept looking through the court records and old reports, I noticed something that couldn't be ignored: Doug's attorneys. These weren't overworked public defenders. They were respected names in Harris County, lawyers who appeared regularly in high-profile cases.

That discovery raised a completely new line of questions: how was Doug paying for this? Where was the money coming from? Was it family connections? Friends in the right places? Who was investing in keeping him out of prison? Or something else entirely? It wasn't just luck. It was clear that Doug had access to legal resources that most people in his situation would never have been able to afford.

That thread mattered to the investigation because it shifted the focus from Doug alone to the ecosystem that enabled him. It wasn't just about his crimes. It was about who helped him slip through the cracks, and why.

I didn't have all the answers yet. And honestly, at that point, I wasn't ready to dive into that part of the story. There was already more than enough to process. Understanding how Doug's legal defenses were handled would have to wait until I could put all the pieces together in a way that made sense.

For now, it was enough to recognize that privilege had played a big role in allowing Doug to slip through the cracks for so long. Without those powerful lawyers steering his cases, without the right people in his corner, things might have turned out very differently.

Now that I had three cases with tangible evidence, it gave a clearer road map of the trail I had to follow. The rape of the minor child in 1974, the assault of Buddy and Learlene Giese, and the attack on my birth mother, Sybil. These weren't just whispers anymore. They were documented. They were real. They were staring me straight in the face.

While these cases were solid anchors, it was Sybil's case that haunted me. It struck me hard that her attack wasn't documented through police reports. If it hadn't been for bits and pieces – family whispers, my Aunt Anita's diary, Sybil's medical records – there would have been no trace of her attack at all.

The fact that I might never have found any proof at all shook me. I realized that relying only on official channels like police records or court cases wouldn't be enough. Official documents were only one layer of the truth.

That thought changed my whole approach. I began to dig deeper and look wider. Police records were only part of the story. I needed to look at cold case files, newspaper archives, missing persons' reports, family testimony, and anything that could reveal hidden patterns. If Sybil's assault had nearly disappeared into silence, how many others had, too?

What about the ones lost completely?

What about the women who never reported anything out of fear, shame, or a sense of futility?

What about the cases where evidence was too slim to record properly, where no one had fought hard enough to keep the files alive?

There was no way to put a real number to it. That realization was almost worse than anything else.

Doug had slipped through the cracks because of more than just good attorneys and leniency. He relied on silence. He relied on shame. He relied on victims who were too afraid, too broken, or too unheard to leave a trace. And the system delivered exactly what he needed – gaps, omissions, and second chances.

The more I pieced together, the angrier I became. His crimes weren't an accident. They weren't isolated lapses in judgment. They formed a consistent, deliberate pattern over time. Doug hurt people because he could, and because no one had ever stopped him.

Each piece I uncovered wasn't just a record of what Doug had done. It was a map of how he'd managed to keep doing it.

The DUIs showed recklessness.

The thefts, opportunism.

The impersonation, manipulation, and control.

The stabbing, raw violence.

The 1974 rape, predation.

The reduced charge, systemic failure.

The high-powered lawyers, privilege, and protection.

Sybil's silence in the records, the cost of being unheard.

Piece by piece, the investigation was forming a narrative that was impossible to ignore. Doug's life wasn't a series of mistakes. It was a blueprint of escalation, supported by silence and privilege.

It wasn't enough anymore to just look at what I knew. I had to consider what I didn't know – the missing pieces, the gaps in the record. Each cold case I found, each missing girl whose story fit just a little too well, widened the scope of what he might have been capable of.

The brutality didn't always leave clear fingerprints. Doug had been smart about it. He picked his moments carefully. He chose situations where victims were isolated, where people might doubt their stories, and authorities could shrug and move on to easier cases.

And when the system did catch up to him, he had the best legal defense money could buy. Lawyers who could twist charges, reduce sentences, and make serious crimes disappear into technicalities. It was never about innocence. It was about privilege and access to the kinds of legal resources that most victims couldn't hope to fight against.

When I found the documentation about his 1974 arrest – the one involving the rape of a minor – I couldn't believe how easily it had been softened. Reduced from an intentional violent rape charge to *"indecency with a child."* One year in jail, with credit for time served. It was sickening.

And it made me wonder how many other cases had followed the same playbook. Quiet negotiations behind closed doors. Charges altered. Sentences lightened. Records buried deep enough that no one would stumble across them by accident.

Doug's ability to move through life unpunished wasn't because he was careful. It was because he was protected.

The deeper I looked into the 1970s era of Doug's life, the more that truth kept rising to the surface. Time and again, he was given a second chance. And a third. Always another opportunity to start fresh. Always another victim who wouldn't get that same grace.

The pattern was undeniable as I built out the timeline, pinning attacks against addresses, dates, and jobs. He had moved around within Texas frequently during that time. Jobs here and there. Temporary housing. New girlfriends, new acquaintances. There was not a lot of stability, but just enough cover to make tracking him difficult.

As I matched each assault to places Doug had lived – Houston, La Marque, Texas City, Galveston, Freeport – the geography itself became evidence. His trail wasn't just in paper records. It was in the map of Texas towns where he lived, worked, and left damage behind.

Deep inside me, I felt like there could be more. I had documented proof of three assaults. But would a serial predator stop there?

The question had shifted entirely. It wasn't *Was Doug violent?* It wasn't even *Was he a repeat offender?*

The question was: *How many victims?*

And worse: *How many would I never be able to name?*

That was the weight of the investigation. Each discovery pulled me deeper, not only into Doug's past, but into the failures of the systems around him. And the deeper I went, the more determined I became.

Because at that point, there was no turning back. The only choice left was to keep digging.

Chapter 8: Built on Circumstance

Once I had confirmed the truth behind three attacks, the line between fact and suspicion began to blur. Each proven case felt like a key turning a larger, locked door – one that opened into a chilling maze of unanswered questions. There were other assaults buried in old reports and whispered memories where the evidence was thin, but the patterns were impossible to ignore. Time, place, and brutality all seemed to echo the same name. The man I had just learned could be my father.

The 1970s had been his playground. And no one had really stopped him. I spent hours combing through websites, public databases, and court archives. Most of the time, it felt like grasping at air. Details were often too vague. Records were incomplete. Names and faces were blurred by time. But then, two cases stood out.

Both of them felt too close to Doug's known behavior to ignore.

The first unsolved case I found that carried striking similarities to Sybil's assault was the murder of Gayle Ann Cater. Gayle was a beautiful 27-year-old woman with long blonde hair who lived at 670 Maxey Road in Houston. At the time, Sybil was living just a mile away at 527 Wood Vista. The proximity was chilling. Two young, blonde women, living so close, attacked within weeks of each other – it felt impossible to ignore.

On Saturday, September 30, 1978, Gayle dropped off her 1973 green Dodge Dart with a white vinyl top at a nearby tune-up shop. After leaving her car, she was last seen walking back to her apartment between 2:00 and 3:00 p.m. She wore blue jeans and a white shirt and carried a large, baggy-type purse. Later that afternoon, around 5:00 p.m., the shop called her apartment to tell her that her car was ready. But when they tried to reach her, the line was busy.

At the same time, Gayle was supposed to have a date with a man named Gary Holt later that night. According to the family, Gary was married at the time and was going through a separation. Gary tried to call Gayle before their 9:00 p.m. date, but the line kept going busy. Concerned, he contacted the phone company. They confirmed the line was working, but it was off the hook. Something wasn't right.

When Gary arrived at Gayle's apartment that night around 9:00 p.m., he found the gate to her complex open. More unsettling, the patio door to her unit was wide open, and when he stepped inside, he saw that the telephone was off the hook, just as the phone company had indicated. Gayle's belongings appeared untouched – her purse was there, along with other personal items – but she was gone. Oddly, her car, which should have been picked up hours earlier, was still parked across the street at the tune-up shop.

On Sunday, October 1, 1978, Gayle's mother, Donna Mae Kennedy – known affectionately as MeeMaw Kennedy – filed a missing person's report with the Harris County Sheriff's Office. It was eventually transferred to the Houston

Police Department. Gayle Cater was now officially listed as missing.

The following morning, October 2, brought a grim discovery. Herbert Caps, a local fisherman, was at his usual spot at the intake locks in a canal in Chambers County, about thirty miles east of Gayle's apartment. Something unusual caught his eye as he cast his lines – a body floating face-up in the water. Authorities from the Chambers County Sheriff's Office responded quickly, and the body was soon identified as Gayle Ann Cater.

She was nude. She had been sexually assaulted. The autopsy revealed manual strangulation as the cause of death, along with crushing injuries to her chest and abdomen – clear signs of a violent attack. Toxicology reports came back negative for alcohol, barbiturates, and narcotics. Gayle hadn't been drugged; she had been overpowered.

The case was handed over to the Houston Police Department's Homicide Division. They worked it diligently, but no suspect was ever formally developed. Gayle's killer walked free, and the case slowly cooled.

Years later, in May 2012, Joseph and I visited Gayle's mother, MeeMaw Kennedy, in Houston. Time had not dulled her pain. MeeMaw greeted us warmly, but you could see the weight she carried in her eyes. Desperation for answers had driven her, even decades after her daughter's murder.

MeeMaw shared with us that at one point, she had visited a psychic, grasping for anything that could lead her closer to the truth. The psychic told her she would find her answers during a month beginning with the letter "M" – March, May. MeeMaw clung to that fragile thread of hope. It might sound far-fetched to some, but no clue seems too small to follow when you're a mother without answers.

We talked for hours. MeeMaw told us about Gayle's life, her relationships, and the people who moved in and out of her world during her final months. Gayle had previously dated her high school sweetheart for some time. According to one of Gayle's best friends, he had a temper. He had an alibi and was ruled out as a suspect.

As I listened to MeeMaw share these painful memories, another possibility loomed in my mind, one she hadn't considered.

Doug.

I couldn't shake the gnawing feeling that my biological father could have been responsible for Gayle's assault and murder. The parallels were too many and too close to ignore. Gayle and Sybil – both beautiful, blonde, young women – both abducted from the same area in East Houston. Both attacks took place within weeks of each other.

I kept going back to Gayle's car – left at the tune-up shop. If Doug had spotted her walking alone, it would have been the perfect opportunity. He was bold enough to take risks, especially ones he thought he could control. And if he already had a method for gaining women's trust, posing as a Good Samaritan or simply overpowering them, it wouldn't have been difficult for him to lure Gayle into a trap.

The location where Gayle's body was found – thirty miles from her home – also pointed to a perpetrator with access to a car, time, and confidence. Doug had all three. The use of strangulation, the calculated disposal of her body, and the lack of forensic evidence left behind were hallmarks of someone who knew how to avoid getting caught.

As more pieces fit together, Gayle's case no longer looked random to me. It looked personal. It looked practiced.

Doug's pattern wasn't one of sudden impulse. It was a trail of carefully executed acts of violence masked by everyday normalcy. He knew how to move through people's lives without leaving obvious marks.

But now, decades later, as I mapped the timeline, the neighborhoods, the victims – his fingerprints were everywhere if you knew how to look.

Gayle Ann Cater's story deserved more than to be another cold case file gathering dust. She deserved justice. Her family deserved answers. And if Doug was responsible, exposing his crimes wouldn't just be about bringing him to light – it would be about honoring every life he destroyed.

In digging deeper into Gayle's case, something unexpected surfaced – something that made my stomach twist. During the course of the investigation, it was discovered that another woman had been abducted, brutally assaulted, and brought to the same general area, the canal where Gayle had been discovered. This attack happened in October 1978, falling almost directly between the attacks on Gayle and Sybil.

It wasn't just the timing that felt significant. It was the location, the method, and the audacity of it all. Whoever had committed these crimes wasn't a man who acted on impulse once. He was comfortable. He was confident. He was, in every sense, hunting.

Joseph and I arranged to visit detectives in Chambers County, hoping to find out more. Texas is an open records state, and we thought that might work in our favor. Despite the passage of many years, this particular case was still classified as active. Because of that, the files were locked away – protected from public eyes, even from families like Gayle's who still lived in hope of answers.

Still, the detectives shared what they could. We learned that the victim in question had eventually passed away, though not immediately after her attack. Her death had come later, but her case remained connected to the events of 1978. Whether her passing was linked to the trauma she endured or some other cause, the detectives did not say. Perhaps they didn't know. Or perhaps, even after all these years, they knew more than they were allowed to tell.

Through additional research and the work documented on the HoustonUnsolved website, a clearer picture of that terrible night began to form. The woman, whose name was not publicly released, had been on foot in the same part of town where Gayle was last seen. It was a stretch of road that, while not completely isolated, had long patches of desolation – perfect for someone who didn't want to be seen.

The attacker pulled up in a blue Ford pickup truck. He leveled a shotgun at the woman and barked at her to do exactly as he said. It was the kind of move that suggested experience. He knew the threat of a gun would strip a victim of her options and force obedience through terror before she had the chance to fight back or flee.

He told her he was from Alabama and had been living in Texas for six years. That detail stuck with me. It was casual, almost conversational. It was as if he was trying to create some kind of false familiarity that might make his victim feel less panicked – or at least compliant. It suggested that this wasn't his first abduction. It suggested that he was practiced at managing fear.

Despite the terror she must have been feeling, somehow, even after being sexually assaulted, this woman managed to escape. Whether she fought, ran, or tricked him remains unclear. What mattered most was that she lived. She got away from a man who had clearly intended for her not to.

A crucial piece of this story caught my attention. The woman was taken to the same general area where Gayle Cater's body was found. A canal in Chambers County.

But even with her escape, no suspect was ever arrested. No one was identified. The blue Ford pickup disappeared into Houston and Harris County traffic sprawl. The man, whoever he was, melted back into his life without consequence.

The similarities between this attack, Gayle's disappearance, and Sybil's brutal assault were impossible to ignore. The proximity of the crimes, the victims' profiles, the method of abduction – it all screamed connection. If Doug was involved in one, it was reasonable to believe he could have been involved in the others.

Doug had lived in Houston at the time. He had a known pattern of violence toward women. He was comfortable around weapons. And he had a particular fixation on women who resembled Sybil – young, blonde, vibrant. These weren't random acts. These were selections.

As I sat with the details, I couldn't help but think about the truck. Doug had driven several different vehicles over the years. Was one of them a blue Ford pickup back in 1978? Had anyone bothered to track that detail at the time? It was the kind of thing that could have been easily overlooked, especially when leads were scarce and technology was primitive compared to today.

The case files on the unidentified woman remained sealed. Without access to the full police reports or her direct statement, I could only speculate about the deeper connection. But in my gut, it felt clear: the timeline, the method, and the victimology fit Doug's evolving pattern.

Still, speculation wasn't enough. I needed more.

Joseph and I kept digging through whatever public records and online archives we could access. We cross-referenced the information with missing persons reports, car thefts, unsolved assaults, and murders from that same time and area. We even reached out to amateur sleuth communities who had been working cold cases from Houston in the late '70s, hoping that someone, somewhere, might have a lead that had been buried or dismissed decades earlier.

In every conversation, one thing was undeniable: this was not an isolated incident. Whoever attacked that unidentified woman had been confident enough to try in broad daylight. He had taken the time to point a gun, give her orders, and try to subdue her. It was only through sheer determination – and maybe a stroke of luck – that she had escaped.

It made me wonder how many others hadn't. How many cases of missing persons from that time might have connections that were never made? How many bodies were found and never linked to one another because the assumption was that these were separate crimes committed by separate people?

The more we uncovered, the more chilling the realization became. Doug and men like him thrived in that environment. An environment where cases were often siloed by jurisdiction, where technology limited the sharing of information, and where women's cases – especially those involving assault – were too often dismissed or not taken seriously enough.

The unidentified woman who escaped that night wasn't just lucky. She was a survivor of a system that had almost been designed to fail her. And while she eventually passed away years later, her courage in surviving that encounter mattered. It mattered for Gayle. It mattered for Sybil. It mattered for every woman who never made it home.

Though her name wasn't known to me, her story had become part of the larger picture. A picture that kept getting sharper with every thread Joseph and I pulled.

And so, with the memory of Gayle, Sybil, and the unidentified survivor heavy in my mind, I kept going.

There was still more to uncover.

In pulling together the threads from Gayle Ann Cater's case, the unidentified survivor's story, and the attacks on Sybil, something unmistakable began to form: a pattern.

And it wasn't subtle.

By this point, there were three confirmed, documented cases of sexual assault tied to the same window of time – and all of them pointed to the same style of predator. The first known incident stretched back to 1974 when Doug sexually assaulted a minor. That case was on record. It wasn't a rumor or an assumption – it was a fact. A child had been hurt, and Doug had been the one responsible.

Fast forward four years to 1978, and suddenly, the violence wasn't just continuing – it was escalating.

My birth mother, Sybil, was attacked in October of that year. She was abducted, assaulted, beaten, and left for dead. Somehow, against all odds, she survived. Her strength saved her life, but the trauma of what she endured would never fully leave her.

Just two months later, in December 1978, another woman – Learlene Gilbert Giese – would fall victim. Doug assaulted her as well, and the brutality of it matched the violence Sybil had suffered.

Three women. Three attacks. Three lives were forever changed because of the actions of one man.

But what if the list didn't stop there?

There were two additional cases that, while not confirmed by formal conviction, carried chilling similarities and enough circumstantial evidence to be impossible to dismiss. Gayle Ann Cater, whose body was found dumped in a canal, and the unidentified woman who somehow survived her encounter formed a grim pattern that couldn't be ignored.

The canal. That's when something snapped in my memory. I had seen that word before. It was mentioned not once, but twice in the police report filed by Buddy and Learlene Giese. Once, Doug had told Buddy, "I could kill you, throw you in a *canal*, and get away with it."

Then, Doug had later threatened Learlene when he said, "If you leave the apartment, Buddy is dead. I will knock him in the head and throw him in the *canal*."

Gayle, Sybil, and the unidentified woman were all abducted from the same general area in Houston. The attacks happened within weeks of each other – in October 1978. Not years apart. Not different regions. The same streets. The same hunting grounds.

It was clear that whoever was behind these assaults wasn't moving randomly. He knew the area. He understood the vulnerabilities in the community – the spots where a woman walking alone could be isolated in a matter of seconds, where screams might be muffled by the endless hum of traffic and city noise.

In Sybil's case, she had been left for dead after being assaulted by multiple men. In Gayle's case, she was murdered and thrown into the murky waters of Chambers County. The unidentified woman had escaped, but barely. Each case was brutally efficient, like someone fine-tuning their method as they went.

And then there was the blue truck.

Witnesses and the surviving victim described the vehicle as a blue Ford pickup. It wasn't just a detail; it was a signature. A mobile trap. The man driving it had a shotgun pointed directly at his victims to force them into compliance. And he had a backstory ready – a casual line dropped like it meant nothing. He told the woman he was from Alabama and had been in Texas for six years.

It seemed like an odd thing for an attacker to share unless you considered it part of his manipulation. A way to humanize himself just enough to make his victims think twice about running. Maybe even make them hesitate just long enough for him to gain total control.

But that "six years" detail wasn't random.

If he had arrived in Texas six years prior to 1978, that would have put his move around 1972. Family members had confirmed that Doug left Alabama and relocated to Houston around that time. He would have been 21 or 22 years old – a young man, already shaped by the dysfunction and violence that clung to him throughout his life.

The pieces fit too well to be a coincidence.

Doug's relocation timeline, the style of attacks, the locations, and the victim profiles – all lined up. Young women, mostly alone, abducted at gunpoint, sexually assaulted, beaten, or killed. The sheer brutality wasn't the act of someone snapping in a moment of rage. It was the behavior of a man who had been operating without fear of being caught.

For the first time, I started to understand why my birth mother might have been targeted.

The victims weren't random. They were selected. And when you looked at the women – Sybil, Gayle, the unidentified survivor – there was a devastating thread connecting them. They were all vulnerable in one way or another. Young, trusting, alone at the wrong moment.

But it was more than opportunity. It was personal.

Sybil wasn't just a random woman walking down a street in Houston. Someone who represented a different kind of prize. The level of violence inflicted on her suggested a rage that ran deeper than simple predation. It hinted at resentment, control, and maybe even revenge.

Doug didn't just want to hurt women. He wanted to dominate them – to erase their autonomy, their choices, and their voices. He wanted power.

Gayle Ann Cater's abduction and murder showed that when dominance alone wasn't enough, death became the ultimate control.

And the unidentified woman who escaped? She had disrupted that control. She hadn't followed the silent script he wrote for his victims. She got away – and that must have enraged her attacker.

Understanding this pattern didn't bring comfort. It brought a cold, relentless kind of clarity.

Doug operated like a hunter who knew exactly what he was doing. He selected victims carefully. He used manipulation, intimidation, and violence with precision. He stayed in areas where he knew the terrain and could disappear into the folds of working-class Houston neighborhoods that barely registered the face of a stranger passing through.

And there was no doubt in my mind that Doug had refined his tactics starting from that first recorded attack on the minor in 1974. Four years later, he was more brutal, efficient, and dangerous.

His move from Alabama to Texas wasn't a clean start. It was a new hunting ground.

Each piece of evidence layered over the next, building a picture of a man who didn't stop because no one had made him stop. A man who would have continued hurting women as long as he could. A man whose actions left scars that reached far beyond his immediate victims.

Doug didn't leave random destruction. He left a trail.

As I sat there with the files, the interviews, and the reports spread around me, I realized something else: Gayle, Sybil, and the unidentified survivor had each fought in their own way. Sybil survived. The unidentified woman escaped. Gayle's family refused to let her name be forgotten.

They had all fought against being erased.

And now it was my turn.

The pattern was clear. The victims were real. Their stories demanded to be seen, not buried under decades of silence.

But the truth refused to stay silent.

Still, even as the facts settled into place, I couldn't stop myself from circling back to one question:

What if?

What if the original felony charge – the rape of a child in 1974 – had stuck?

What if Doug had been held accountable back then, before he was allowed to slip through the cracks?

I couldn't help but think about how many futures would have been spared the wreckage he left behind.

Callie's cousin, Learlene Gilbert Giese, might have been saved from the unimaginable trauma she endured.

She could have been spared. Her life could have unfolded differently – free from the pain, the scars, the stolen sense of safety that Doug inflicted.

And then my mind would turn, without permission, to Sybil.

What if Sybil had been spared, too?

What if, on that October day in 1978, she had never crossed paths with Doug and the two other men who brutalized her?

How different would her life have been?

Would she have found peace? Would she have built a different future, one not shaped by trauma and survival?

It's a haunting thought because Sybil's attack didn't just alter her path – it created mine.

If Doug and the others hadn't hurt her, I would not exist.

It's an impossible tightrope to walk.

How do you weigh one life against another?

How do you ask whose existence carries more weight – the mother who survived unthinkable violence or the son born because of it?

There's no fair answer. No clean way to make sense of it.

Sybil's life was shattered that night. She carries the pieces with her, even today.

And yet, from those broken pieces, my life was formed.

It's not lost on me that every moment I breathe, every step I take, is tied to something she never should have had to endure.

I owe my life to her strength, endurance, and refusal to let the darkness consume her.

And still, if I could have spared her the pain – even at the cost of my own existence – wouldn't that have been the right thing?

Wouldn't it have been justice?

These questions have no satisfying answer.

They live in the gray spaces where morality, fate, and survival tangle themselves into knots too tight to undo.

Some days, I can sit with the complexity of it. I can accept that life, as cruel as it sometimes is, doesn't follow the rules of fairness or logic.

On other days, its weight feels unbearable.

The thought that my life is a ripple from someone else's suffering… it's a heavy thing to carry.

But here's what I do know, with absolute certainty:

Sybil's life mattered.

Gayle Ann Cater's life mattered.

The unidentified woman's life mattered.

Learlene Gilbert Giese's life mattered.

The minor child's life mattered.

They were not just victims. They were women with hopes, dreams, families, and futures they deserved to see fulfilled.

And while I can't rewrite the past – can't undo the failures of a justice system that let Doug slip away – I can refuse to let their stories be forgotten.

I can stand the truth, even when it hurts.

Especially when it hurts.

Because their lives were more than the worst things that happened to them.

And my life, born from the ashes of Sybil's pain, carries the responsibility of honoring that truth.

Not by pretending the pain didn't exist.

Not by tying it up in platitudes.

But by telling their stories fully, fiercely, and without apology.

Their truth demands it.

And so does mine.

Chapter 9: Confirmation

Joseph and I met in 2009 at a small church in Houston. At the time, he was managing the Social Security office in Bryan, Texas – a quiet town with just enough bustle to keep life moving but not so much that it ever felt overwhelming. In 2011, we bought our first home together in Bryan. It was modest but warm, and it quickly became the place where we built our first real rhythm as a couple.

That house in Bryan was also the backdrop for one of the most complicated chapters of my life. It was there I first spoke with Doug by phone in the spring of 2012. And it was where our last conversation unfolded – the final call, the final words. Contact with Doug and some of the Williams family seemed to fade shortly after. No dramatic ending, just a slow and steady silence that stretched itself over days, then weeks, then months.

But silence didn't bring peace. That same house, with its familiar creaks and corners, became the place where the night terrors returned. They didn't sneak up gently. They hit hard – violent jolts in the middle of the night, waking up in a panic, heart racing, drenched in sweat. I'd wake up screaming, sometimes running down the hallway before I even knew I was out of bed. It was as if my body remembered something my conscious mind couldn't fully access.

Thankfully, that house in Bryan was also where I found help. A local therapist – compassionate, patient, and unafraid of digging deep – helped me start the long process of unraveling the trauma I had kept buried for too long. Little by little, the terrors softened. They didn't vanish overnight, but their grip loosened. Eventually, they became less frequent. When they surfaced, they came with less fury. An occasional yell in the dark, not a full sprint through the house. It was progress.

Life, as it does, kept moving forward. Joseph's career gave us new opportunities, and in September 2012, we relocated to Dallas. It was a major transition – selling one house, buying another, navigating new streets, and meeting new neighbors. I had to find a new job, of course, but with my background in banking and finance, I managed to land on my feet quickly. The change of scenery gave us a fresh start. But even as life was filled with to-do lists and career goals, one thing never really left my mind: the question of Doug.

Communication with him had gone silent. Every lead I had explored had led me into a fog. I wasn't actively investigating anymore – there just wasn't time – but the weight of that unresolved question stayed with me, gnawing at the edges of my peace.

What if I never knew for sure?

My gut told me Doug was my biological father. Everything pointed in that direction. But instincts aren't proof. I needed something tangible – something that couldn't be denied or debated. There were the stories, of course: confirmed sexual assault cases during that same period,

Doug's long record of run-ins with the law. Then there was the timing. The location. The eerie pattern kept circling back to him.

Still, the doubt lingered.

What if I was wrong?

Doug had never admitted to anything. He'd consistently denied even the possibility, not just to me, but to anyone who brought it up. He brushed it off like a ridiculous rumor. A fantasy someone had made up to cause trouble.

All I had was a mountain of circumstantial evidence.

There was the page from Aunt Anita's diary that she had ripped out and given to me, hinting at secrets nobody wanted to speak aloud.

The Y-DNA match from FamilyTreeDNA was an undeniable link that tied me to Doug's family line, proving a genetic relationship, though it stopped short of confirming him specifically.

There were court records. Arrest reports. Police documents from various counties and states, each piece adding to the same picture: a man with a pattern of violating boundaries, of crossing lines, of hurting others. There were so many names that could be connected to him, even if the courts had never quite managed to tie them all together.

Sybil's medical records were also included. Documents that described the brutal attack she endured from three unidentified men. Details that never made it into a courtroom but lived on in hospital files and therapist notes.

Yet, with all of that, I still had no direct proof. No DNA from Doug himself. No signed paternity acknowledgment. No piece of paper that said, without question, "This is your father."

That lack of certainty became its own wound because of what it meant for my identity, and what it meant for everyone else – for Sybil, Gayle, and the unidentified woman who escaped. If I couldn't prove he was my father, then I couldn't prove he had assaulted Sybil. And if I couldn't prove that, how could I connect him to the other victims? How could I hold him accountable for the lives he shattered?

Every now and then, I'd try to convince myself that maybe it didn't matter. Maybe what mattered most was that I knew the truth in my bones, even if I couldn't put it in writing. But that kind of mental gymnastics only worked for a while. Deep down, I wanted something irrefutable. Something that didn't leave space for doubt, denial, or dismissal.

Until I had it, I wasn't done.

Life had other plans.

In September 2014, Joseph accepted a new position as the district manager for the Social Security office in Texarkana, Texas. It was another big move – another chapter. We sold our condo in Dallas, packed up our lives, and began the familiar process of relocation. For 63 days, we lived in temporary housing while we waited to close on a home in Texarkana. It wasn't glamorous, but it was manageable. After doing this a few times, I had gotten used to the moving boxes, short-term addresses, and quick job applications that followed each new zip code.

Once we settled into our new home, life returned to a steady rhythm. Joseph dove into his new role. I found work again in finance and banking – my comfort zone. We adjusted quickly. For a few years, I barely touched my research. I told myself I'd gone as far as I could. There weren't any new leads to chase or names to investigate. I had hit a plateau. There wasn't anything left to dig into that wouldn't feel like retracing steps.

Then, in March 2018, we planned a long-overdue family vacation. Joseph, Callie, and I mapped out a nine-day trip to the East Coast. It was a well-thought-out journey, where each stop brought us face-to-face with cousins and extended family members we hadn't seen in years, or had only ever spoken to over the phone. It wasn't labeled a reunion, but that's what it became. One of Callie's cousins joked, "Y'all did a whole family reunion, one cousin at a time!"

And it was true. It was one of those rare trips that fed your soul and fostered a real sense of connection. It reminded me how important family really is. But something else unexpected happened on that trip – something I hadn't planned for.

Up until then, I had only met two people from my paternal side of the family. First, Doug, of course, back in 2012, during that short window when we briefly spoke. Around that same time, I'd had a chance to meet one of his sisters, Mary Bazan. She lived north of Dallas, and while our interaction had been brief, it had meant something to me. Those two meetings, though small, were all I had.

Now, in Asheville, North Carolina, that changed. While staying there for a few days during the trip, I met Gordon Johnson – my second cousin. We had arranged to meet for dinner, and I was both nervous and excited. Gordon, like his mother, had a deep love for family history. He brought pictures, photo albums, and decades of stories. We laughed over old photos, and he shared details about relatives I had only read about in documents or seen in scanned copies of records.

That dinner with Gordon wasn't just a nice night out – it was something more. It felt like a reconnection. A small but meaningful restoration of a branch of family I had long felt severed from. It had been six years since I had met Doug and Mary. Six years of silence. And here was Gordon, sitting across the table, not just sharing a meal but offering a piece of my history. It wasn't closure, but it was a step forward.

Our life in Texarkana carried on. For five years, we made a home there. We built routines. We made friends. We adjusted to the slower pace of the town. Life was steady, even good.

Then came another shift.

In September 2019, Joseph was offered another relocation opportunity – this time back to Dallas, where he took a position managing the Dallas North Social Security Office. By now, we had a system. Pack up. Sell the house. Buy a new one. Rebuild from scratch. We found a new home in Garland, Texas, just outside the city. I updated my resume and began the job hunt again. What once felt overwhelming now just felt routine.

But this move came with additional challenges.

Every house Joseph and I had bought – Bryan, Dallas, Texarkana – had always had separate living quarters for Callie. Sometimes she would stay with us on occasion, and then she would return home or travel around the country.

During this move, Callie's health had started to decline. She moved with us to Garland so we could help care for her. The three of us settled into our new surroundings. We were just beginning to feel at home again when everything came to a grinding halt.

COVID-19.

The pandemic changed everything overnight. The structure we had rebuilt began to shift under our very feet. Like so many others, Joseph and I transitioned to remote work. We hunkered down, avoided gatherings, and distanced ourselves from loved ones – not out of choice, but necessity. The world had changed, and we had to adapt.

During that time, my research once again took a back seat. The demands of life had always pulled me away from it before, but this was different. The pressure of daily life and the pandemic's isolation left little space for digging into the past. Most days were about getting through work, checking on Callie, and keeping ourselves healthy.

There was no emotional bandwidth for chasing shadows.

Still, the unresolved questions never fully disappeared. They just went quiet for a while.

Then, another breakthrough.

Sometime in 2020, while we were adjusting to the slow and uncertain rhythm of pandemic life, I received a message that caught me completely off guard. I had connected with a first cousin – Doug's niece. We had never spoken before, and never even crossed paths. She was the daughter of Mary Bazan, Doug's sister – the same Mary who had met Joseph and me for lunch back in 2012.

I remembered that meeting well. Mary had been kind, reserved, and open to getting to know me. She had been the only person in Doug's family who had really remained in contact with him over the years. Unlike some others, she hadn't cut him off entirely, despite the distance Doug had created for himself.

Doug had always been a bit of a mystery. Or maybe more accurately, a storm people had learned to avoid. My cousin told me that much of the family had stayed distant from Doug. There were no real connections anymore – just silence. According to her, "Since my mother passed away, no one in the family has really heard from Doug. We are unsure if he is even alive."

It stopped me in my tracks.

I hadn't heard from him either, not since that last phone call.

It had been eight long years. Still, I could hear his voice like it was yesterday. That final conversation wasn't something I could forget even if I tried. The rage in his tone. The way he'd barked those words at me – "Bring it on, Buddy! Bring it on!" I could still feel their weight. That moment marked the end of our communication, and I had no idea what had happened after.

So, when my cousin said they didn't know if Doug was even alive, I didn't know how to respond. Part of me didn't want to know.

Did I really want to open that door again?

I wasn't sure, but the conversation stirred something in me. Not because I thought it would lead to an emotional reconciliation or tie everything up in a bow – but because I still didn't have answers and that itch for understanding had never really gone away.

It wasn't about building a relationship with Doug anymore. It was about clarity.

If this really was the last door that could be opened, I had to try. I had to know whether that chapter was finished or just incomplete.

The conversation felt like a breath of fresh air. Even though it didn't give me immediate answers, it reminded me I wasn't entirely alone on this journey. Someone else on the paternal side of my family had reached out. Someone with a real connection to the same people I had been researching for years. For so long, I had been operating in silence. Now, I had someone who was willing to talk.

She had few answers, but she was open and willing to listen. That meant something.

I saw this as my window – not just to possibly find out what happened to Doug, but also to reignite the research I had quietly put away. I dusted off the old folders. I opened up the digital files I hadn't touched in months and began looking again. Even if it led nowhere, even if Doug remained in the shadows, this was a spark I couldn't ignore.

After nearly a decade of fractured communication and unfinished questions, it finally felt like a path was opening again – even if it was just a narrow one.

During my searches, I found a phone number listed for Doug. After a long period of contemplating whether I really wanted to make contact again – I dialed the number.

"Hello." The voice on the other end of the line was Alice Luna.

Alice was a surprising discovery. She wasn't someone I had expected to come across – her name hadn't appeared in any earlier records or conversations. I later learned she had played a significant role in Doug's life. From what I could piece together, Doug had met Alice sometime shortly after he was released from prison in 2005.

At the time, Doug was around 55 years old. Alice was 78. The idea that these two very different people – living very different lives – would somehow form a deep and lasting friendship seemed improbable. Yet, they had. And it all started in the most unlikely of places.

Doug had always had a thing for slot machines. Gambling gave him a kind of high that seemed to satisfy a part of his restless nature. But Texas isn't known for its abundance of legal gambling venues, and it wasn't easy to find a spot where he could indulge in his favorite pastime. Still, there was one place he frequented – a small convenience store tucked away in Houston, near where Doug was living at the time. In the back of the store was a room with a handful of slot machines – low-key, off the radar, and mostly visited by locals who didn't mind operating in gray areas.

Doug and Alice had met in that convenient store.

Alice Luna, as I later learned, was a unique individual. A gifted artist with a youthful energy that defied her age. Even well into her 90s, she continued to paint. As I would see later, her work was full of life and color, much like her personality. She had this huge smile, a high-spirited way of speaking, and a strong presence. She didn't seem like the kind of person you could easily fool.

Their relationship started off simple enough. Just two people crossing paths at a small-time slot room. But over time, something more developed – something meaningful. Alice became a kind of mother figure to Doug, who saw beyond his rough exterior and offered help when needed.

She wasn't a pushover, though. Not even close.

Alice was sharp. She could tell the difference between a person down on their luck and someone trying to take advantage. Doug never begged her for anything. He didn't ask for handouts, but Alice had a way of noticing things. She paid attention.

One day, she saw him wearing shoes with holes in them. Doug never mentioned them. He didn't complain. Alice didn't wait for him to ask. She simply brought him to the store and bought him two new pairs. That was how she was – quietly observant, deeply generous, and confident in her instincts.

Their relationship wasn't one-sided either. Doug mowed her lawn. He stopped by often to check on her. He drove her to her doctor's appointments and made sure she had what she needed. In many ways, he became like family to her. A companion. A protector. A help. In return, she supported him when he needed it most.

She even helped him get a car. That car allowed Doug to stay connected to her and, perhaps more importantly, gave him a small sense of independence he hadn't had in years.

It made me wonder.

Had prison changed Doug? Had those years behind bars mellowed him, softened some of the edges that had made him so volatile and aggressive? Or was Alice's influence just bringing out something better in him?

I didn't know, but I could tell from everything I had learned that Doug genuinely cared for her, and Alice clearly cared for him. So, when Alice answered the number I had found for Doug, I wasn't sure what to expect.

"Hi," I said when she picked up the phone. "I'm calling about Douglas Williams. The family hasn't heard from him in some time, and we're worried something might have happened to him. We just want to know if he's okay – if he's still alive."

That was all it took.

Without hesitation, Alice began to speak. Her voice was warm and animated. She didn't hold back. She told me Doug was still alive, but his health wasn't good. His lung cancer had returned. The tone in her voice shifted when she said it. You could hear the concern. The weight of what it meant.

At first, I thought she believed I was just another family member from Alabama, checking in out of concern. It wasn't long into the conversation before I realized that was exactly what she thought.

So, I decided to be honest.

"I need to tell you something," I said. "I think Doug might be my biological father."

There was a pause. It wasn't long, but it was enough to feel.

From that moment on, the way Alice spoke to me changed. Her tone softened, but not in the way I expected. She became more careful. Guarded. Protective.

"I've heard about you," she said.

Then she repeated something I had heard before – word for word.

"Doug can't be your biological father. He was in prison at the time of your conception."

It hit me hard. That same story. The same timeline. Doug had given me the same alibi years ago when I confronted him about our possible connection. He had always claimed he was locked up during that time. I had proof. I had his arrest records, but the way he told the story – calculated, deliberate – always left me with doubt.

Now here was Alice, repeating that exact line.

Alice didn't know me yet; she knew that version of the story as if it were a fact, which meant that Doug had told her about me. At some point in the eight years since we had last spoken, I had come up in a conversation.

Maybe more than once.

That realization was strange. After all the silence, all the anger, all the distance – he had remembered me. He had talked about me. Maybe not kindly. Maybe not accurately. But he hadn't forgotten.

It left me with mixed emotions.

Alice remained kind and polite for the rest of our conversation. She didn't shut down. She didn't hang up. I could feel the shift. She no longer seemed as open as she had at the beginning. She clearly didn't believe I was Doug's son.

Still, before we hung up, she offered to give Doug my phone number. She said she'd pass it along and leave the decision to him.

I thanked her for her time, for her honesty, and for being willing to talk at all. She didn't owe me anything; yet, she had given me something – another piece to the puzzle, even if it didn't fit neatly.

After we ended the call, I sat quietly for a long while.

Would I hear from Doug again?

I didn't know. Part of me hoped I would. Another part wasn't sure what I would even say if he did call.

How do you restart a conversation that ended in shouting nearly a decade earlier? What words would make sense after all that had happened?

I didn't have the answers, but I was one step closer to the truth.

Finding Alice had opened up something I hadn't expected. It didn't bring final closure. It didn't offer clear proof. It gave me a glimpse into Doug's life – the life he had built in the years since our last encounter. A life filled with pain, yes, but also connection. A life where someone like Alice had become important to him, and he to her.

That mattered.

Even if the question of paternity remained unresolved, the truth of Doug's humanity – the reality of who he had become – was no longer hidden in shadows. I had seen a piece of it. I had heard it in Alice's voice.

Somehow, that meant something.

Then it happened!

Within just a few days, my phone rang. My heart skipped a beat when I heard the voice on the other end – Doug. After all the silence, the dead ends, the missed chances, there he was. His voice was different now. He wasn't aggressive or threatening like before. But he wasn't warm or inviting either. He was flat. Cold. Maybe tired. Maybe cautious.

"What do you want?" he asked.

The words weren't angry, but they weren't exactly friendly. It sounded like I had interrupted his day. Like this was a favor he didn't really want to do.

I swallowed hard and kept my voice calm.

"Just checking in. The family hasn't heard from you in a long time. People were concerned. I wanted to see how you're doing."

He responded in a tone that was more detached than anything. He gave me a quick rundown of his health – his cancer had returned, and he was dealing with treatments. He didn't seem emotional about it, just factual, like he was ticking off information from a list. I wasn't sure what I expected, but hearing the reality of his condition, even in that matter-of-fact tone, left me feeling off balance.

At the end of the call, almost by instinct, I said, "You can reach out to me anytime."

I didn't plan those words. They just came out. Maybe it was out of politeness, or maybe some part of me still hoped that if I kept the door open, even just a crack, the truth would eventually come through it.

A few days later, Doug did call back.

That call was different. It still wasn't warm, but it shifted. Somewhere in the middle of the conversation, Doug brought up the one topic I had long given up hope he'd ever mention again.

"I don't think I'm your father," he said, direct and plainspoken, "but I want to help you have closure."

I sat with those words for a second. I couldn't believe what I was hearing. For years, he had refused even to consider the possibility of a DNA or paternity test. I still remember how he had walked out of FamilyTreeDNA in 2012 without ever taking the test. That moment had stayed with me. It was burned into my memory. And now, suddenly, he was saying he would help me get closure?

"I've been looking into how to do it," he continued. "I found a place that does paternity testing."

He was already ahead of me.

This time, Doug was the one setting the terms. He had found the testing company. He had looked into the cost. And he made it clear: he would be the one to pay for it.

I was stunned, but I didn't push back right away. I listened as he explained that because he lived on a fixed income – Social Security and SSI – he wouldn't have the money until the first of the next month. Only then could he pay for the test.

I felt the pressure building in my chest. I didn't want to wait. I knew from experience how quickly he could change his mind.

What if he had a bad day and backed out? What if this was a momentary lapse in his usual guardedness and he'd soon put the walls back up?

"Doug," I said, trying to sound casual even though I was anything but, "I can cover the cost. Really, it's no problem. Let's just do it."

But Doug wouldn't hear of it.

He was firm. He insisted that he would be the one to pay. I started to get the sense that this was about more than money. Maybe he felt like if I paid, I'd somehow take control of the process – or the results. Maybe he didn't want to feel like he owed me anything. Whatever it was, he held his ground.

So, I waited.

Those next few weeks moved at a crawl. Each day felt like a week. I checked my phone constantly. I kept rereading the details Doug had given me. I reminded myself not to get too hopeful.

However, the one thing that gave me a little bit of peace was the fact that Doug kept in touch during the waiting period. He didn't disappear. He didn't go silent. That was new.

In those conversations, Doug started doing something strange. He kept insisting he couldn't be my father. Over and over again, he repeated that he had been in prison at the time of my conception. And then, he began offering up other possibilities.

"I believe your father could be Buddy." he told me.

Known as Buddy, John Henry Williams was Doug's brother. According to Doug, Buddy would pass through Houston from time to time.

Another day, he offered a different name.

"You know," he said, "I think your father is Charles."

Charles Edward Williams was another of Doug's brothers who had served in the military. Doug explained that Charles would visit their sister, Joyce, in Houston every now and then.

Each time we talked, there was a new possibility. A new name. A new theory.

I started to wonder what Doug was doing.

Was he trying to help? Was this genuine brainstorming – or was he planting doubt?

It began to feel like he was carefully creating an environment where I could believe anyone was my father except him. At first, I chalked it up to guilt. Maybe he honestly believed he wasn't my father and just wanted to point me in the right direction. After a while, it started to feel like something else.

Was he deliberately trying to create reasonable doubt? Was this his way of distancing himself again? Laying the groundwork for another retreat, just in case he didn't like the outcome?

I didn't say much. I just listened. I let him talk. I didn't argue. I didn't challenge the names he suggested. But deep inside, the seeds of confusion were starting to sprout.

Could he really not be my father? Was I wrong all along?

I had been so sure. From the first time I met him, my gut had told me that there was something there – some unspoken recognition. But now, I wasn't so sure anymore.

Doug's words started to sink in. They weren't wild or emotional. They were delivered with such calm, such certainty, that it made me question my own memory and instincts.

Yet, there was still that phone call. There was still the fact that he had found the testing center and agreed to take the test. That he was willing to pay.

Whatever his reasons, Doug was finally doing something he had refused to do for years.

It was happening.

The first of the month finally came, and Doug received his checks. Just like he said he would, he followed through. He had already identified the company he wanted to use to conduct the paternity test. It was a DNA Diagnostics Center collection site in Houston – one of the more widely used services, known for its strict chain-of-custody protocols and accurate reporting. Doug scheduled his appointment and went in to test first.

It was surreal to know that this was really happening – after all those years of unanswered questions, that swab against the inside of his cheek would help settle something that had followed me around for most of my life. And I didn't want to leave anything to chance, so I did my own homework.

I looked up the company and read everything I could find on their testing methods, customer reviews, and credibility. I wanted to be sure this wasn't some shady operation. It wasn't. They had been around for decades, used by courts and hospitals, and their reputation had checked out.

With that peace of mind, I made my appointment. My test will be collected at a partner location in Dallas. I showed up, signed the paperwork, let them verify my ID, and took my turn in the chair. The technician handed me the swab and instructed me to rub the inside of my cheek. Just like that – it was done.

The easy part was over.

Now came the waiting, and with the waiting came the weight.

Thousands of emotions ran through my head in the days that followed. The samples had been collected. The lab had received them. Doug's in Houston. Mine in Dallas. They were being tested together. We were now on the same report.

That report was going to change something – either for the better or in a way that would force me to rethink everything I thought I knew.

I told myself to breathe. I told myself to stay calm, but the closer we got to the day, the louder the noise in my head became.

I kept going back and forth. One minute, I felt confident. I had been so sure all these years. The Y-DNA match. The strong resemblance. The family patterns. The circumstantial evidence. My gut. My instincts. All of it pointed to Doug. I had followed the clues like pieces of a puzzle and felt certain I had put them together correctly.

But then, doubt would creep in.

Doug had always been so firm – so unshakable in his denials. He didn't leave room for possibility. He had stories.

Timelines. Locations. Alibis. He said he had been in prison at the time of my conception. He gave specific reasons why it couldn't be him. He never hesitated to suggest someone else: his brother Buddy, his brother Charles, even a cousin. It made me wonder.

What if he really believed it? What if I had built an entire truth around something that wasn't accurate? What if Doug was right?

The doubts ate away at me, growing bigger.

What if it wasn't him – but someone else in the family? Someone who happened to be in Houston at the same time. Someone who crossed paths with my birth mom – Sybil. What if all the patterns I thought I recognized were just coincidences?

If that were the case, I would be back at square one. Again.

The thought made my chest tighten. The idea that I could be this close to the truth, only for it to slip through my fingers again, was overwhelming. I tried to distract myself. Work, chores, anything that would pass the time. But every time I opened my inbox or checked my phone, I was hoping to see that email.

And then – finally – it came.

The email notification lit up my screen: **"Your DNA Paternity Test Results Are Ready."**

My stomach dropped.

I stared at it for a second, knowing that a single click would reveal something I had waited my whole life to know. I took a breath, sat down at my computer, and opened the report.

There it was.

Plain as day.

"99.999996% probability that Douglas 'Doug' Lamar Williams is my biological father."

My eyes locked on that number. I read it. Then read it again. The science was absolute. The margin of error wasn't even worth discussing. This wasn't a maybe. This wasn't a probability worth questioning. This was a fact.

Doug was my father.

The moment hit me hard. Not like a punch, not like a wave – but more like a deep, silent collapse inside me. I had spent over a decade searching, turning over every rock, writing down every name, following every thread.

Wondering. Hoping. Doubting.

Now, here it was.

An answer.

The truth.

It was September 3, 2020. Almost eleven years after Callie had handed me that DNA test for Christmas in 2009. That simple gift had changed everything. That moment, back then, when I had first submitted my sample and matched to a first cousin in Alabama – a man I didn't know at the time, but who I now understood was Doug's nephew – had been the first crack in the wall.

At the time, a Y-DNA match that close was rare. The odds of randomly testing and matching a cousin that closely, especially across state lines like that, were nearly unheard of. But now, with millions of people submitting DNA to companies like Ancestry, 23andMe, FamilyTreeDNA, and others, matches like that are far more common. Back then, it was a rarity. Now, it made sense.

That match was the breadcrumb. That was the trailhead. And every step I took from there – through doubt, silence, resistance, and even rejection – had led me here.

I was now the *Walking Proof* that linked Doug to Sybil.

There was no more wondering. No more back-and-forth. No more manufactured alibis. No more maybe-this-or-that-brother theories. It was Doug. It always had been. The science backed it up.

In that moment, I wasn't angry. I wasn't even emotional in the way I thought I would be when I learned the truth. I didn't cry. I didn't shake. I didn't collapse. Instead, I just sat there, processing it, and I thought about Sybil and what she endured. How her story had been denied, ignored, and buried for so long, and how that one kit – one test – had brought it all into the light.

I thought about Doug and the many years he had refused to talk, take the test, and just refused to face it.

Then I thought about myself.

I had always known.

Somewhere deep inside, I had always known.

This test didn't change anything – it confirmed everything, and this confirmation was a powerful thing. Now, no one could take it away. No one could question it. No one could rewrite it.

It was done.

Chapter 10: An Unconventional Relationship

The weight of the truth hit me fast and hard.

There was no more doubt. No more guesswork. Doug was one of Sybil's rapists and my biological father.

It was a heavy duality to carry – proof of a brutal crime and the origin of my life wrapped into one reality. I didn't know what to do with that. I didn't know how to make sense of the fact that the worst moment of Sybil's life had also created mine.

How do you hold those two truths in the same breath?

I found myself replaying everything that had led me here. I went back to 2009, the year Callie gave me the DNA kit. At the time, it had felt like a fun gift – something new to explore. Then came 2012, the year I met Doug face-to-face for the first time. From the moment I saw him, something had settled in my gut. I didn't need a lab to tell me what I knew. I saw the resemblance. I heard it in his voice.

Still, I pushed for solid evidence. I needed more than instinct. I wanted to be absolutely sure.

Now I was.

By September 2020, there was no denying it. I was the *Walking Proof.* I was the evidence Sybil never got to present in court, but it was in the numbers, science, and every piece of documentation I had gathered over the years. I was the living result of a truth that had been denied, ignored, and buried for decades.

But with the answer in hand, I was left with a different question: Now what?

There was no roadmap for what I was supposed to do next. No guide for how to carry this kind of confirmation. The emotional weight of it didn't come all at once – it came in waves. Some moments were quiet. Others were loud and disorienting. There was no clear beginning or end to the processing.

I couldn't fully explain it to anyone, even when they asked. I didn't have the right words for the kind of weight that presses on your chest when you know the origin of your life is tied to someone else's pain.

I knew justice wouldn't come in any official way. The statute of limitations had long expired. I wasn't naïve about that. There would be no court date, no legal reckoning, no arrest. That didn't mean I didn't feel the need for accountability. It didn't mean I didn't want answers.

That's when the phone started ringing.

Doug began calling. I don't know what had changed on his end. Maybe he felt something shift, or he knew the wall had finally come down, or he was just curious. But the calls came in.

I didn't approach those conversations with hope, and I didn't approach them with anger either. I was measured.

Calm. Focused. I knew what I wanted – and it wasn't a connection. I had no interest in building a relationship with him. That wasn't the point. I wanted clarity. I wanted to study him. Listen. Watch the way he answered. Pay attention to the things he said and the things he didn't. I had spent years wondering who this man really was. Now, I had the chance to observe him for myself.

Each conversation was its own kind of exercise. I wasn't digging for an apology. I didn't expect anything. I just wanted the truth – or at least, as much of it as he was willing to show.

Now that I had confirmation, I wasn't just living with the truth. I was walking with it, day in and day out, like a weight strapped to my chest. It didn't go away. It didn't get lighter. I didn't dwell on it constantly, but it was always there – present in every interaction, every word, every memory.

Doug was cautious in our conversations. Guarded. He measured his words, revealing just enough to keep the exchange going while skillfully dodging anything deeper. He had mastered a kind of verbal self-preservation – concealing, deflecting, and withholding as if it were second nature. For him, it probably was.

We spoke regularly, especially in the early mornings. Doug was up before dawn – every day – by 5:00 a.m. sharp. I'd take his calls on the way to the gym, just before my workday started. The rhythm of those conversations was often bland and repetitive. Small talk. Weather updates. Political opinions. News around his senior living complex.

He'd comment on grocery prices, the mail schedule, or which neighbor had passed away. I listened politely but often disengaged emotionally. As an introvert, I was used to being quiet. These surface-level conversations weren't challenging – they were just draining.

Still, I kept answering.

Every so often, something different slipped in – something real. He would mention family members. Bits and pieces. A sister here. A cousin there. Names I didn't recognize, connections I hadn't made yet. Though Doug had distanced himself from many of them over the years – burned bridges, moved cities, changed numbers – those glimpses into his extended family were meaningful to me.

They helped me piece together the branches of a family tree I had only started to trace. Even if Doug didn't say much, those crumbs mattered. They gave shape to people I'd never met but were technically connected to.

Sometimes he talked about work. His job history was inconsistent and chaotic – a series of gigs with no pattern or long-term security. He had worked on construction crews, offshore oil rigs, tugboats, and delivery trucks. Then he mentioned managing adult bookstores in Houston.

That one caught me off guard.

A registered sex offender working in that kind of environment? It didn't add up. Before I could ask, he explained himself.

"I was paid under the table and worked under an alias," he said casually, like it was no big deal.

But when I tried to dig deeper, he instantly shut down. It was like he realized too late that he had let something slip. He clammed up. The walls went back up. The moment was gone.

Then came a conversation that shook me to my core.

"I've never hurt a woman," Doug said.

He said it plainly, like a fact he'd been rehearsing for years. My entire body tensed. My chest burned. I felt like I had been slapped. For someone who claimed not to remember anything, he sure seemed committed to a version of the story.

I stayed calm, but I didn't let it slide.

"I know exactly what happened to my mother," I said, keeping my voice steady. "I have her medical records. I've seen the police reports. I know she wasn't the only one. We can agree not to discuss it, but you can't pretend it didn't happen."

I told him plainly that I had no plans to expose him while he was alive, but I wouldn't play along with a lie either. I couldn't pretend this wasn't real. I wouldn't let us pretend.

"The statute of limitations has passed," I said, "but if I could press charges and send you back to prison, I would."

Doug didn't protest. He didn't raise his voice. He didn't try to argue.

"That's fair," he said.

Just like that.

It caught me off guard – not because I expected a fight, but because it was so flat, so direct, so unbothered. Maybe it was fear. Maybe he sensed that I was serious and wasn't going to let it drop. Maybe he realized I wasn't trying to blackmail him or destroy him – I just wasn't going to lie for him.

The closest thing to an admission came a few seconds later, when he added, "Well, she was just in the wrong place at the wrong time."

That sentence hung in the air like smoke from a fire long put out, but still lingering.

He never brought it up again. Not once.

After that, things returned to the usual rhythm. Doug would call. We'd talk. He'd mention groceries, the weather, or what he saw on the news. But his tone changed. His voice softened. He never pushed back against anything I said. He was getting older, thinner, and slower. He turned 70 not long after. His breathing had become labored. You could hear it in every word. His voice cracked more often. The sharpness had dulled. He didn't have the same energy he had when we first met eight years earlier.

By then, I no longer feared him – not for myself, not for Joseph. That part of the past had lost its grip. He wasn't the threat he once was. He was just an old man with a weak voice and fading lungs, still holding his secrets while I held the truth.

Doug's world was small. Alice Luna, her family, a few neighbors, a woman who helped clean his apartment, and his church. That was it. At 70, the sudden appearance of a son didn't just disrupt his daily routine – it shook the fragile narrative he had built around himself. He had worked hard to keep the past buried. Now I was here, forcing him to acknowledge a truth he'd spent decades avoiding.

He couldn't tell people the truth: that he had raped and assaulted my mother, and I was the result of that night. So, he lied instead.

"She never told me about him," he told Alice, painting himself as the victim. "I never knew he existed."

Classic victim-blaming. Sybil didn't know who had attacked her. She didn't get the luxury of identifying the men who hurt her. So how could she have told him anything? His lie wasn't just a denial – it was his excuse for being absent, for not reaching out, for choosing not to care. It gave him a narrative that made him look like a man wronged by circumstance, rather than one who created the circumstances to begin with.

Still, we talked. Carefully. Uneasily.

My job required me to be in and out of courthouses. As a manager at a finance company, I filed lawsuits and testified at hearings. Doug called me on one of those routine drives to the courthouse in Dallas. I mentioned going there, without thinking, about where I was headed.

That was enough to trigger his paranoia.

"Why are you going to the courthouse?" he asked, his voice tight. "Is it about me? What are you looking for?"

I was caught off guard. To me, the courthouse was just work. To him, it was a symbol of exposure and of judgment. His fear that I might be digging into his past caused him to spiral. And once he started unraveling, the floodgates opened.

"I worked with law enforcement in the 1970s," he said suddenly, almost as if the words had been waiting decades to escape. "They used me to plant drugs or intimidate people who owed debts. I'm nobody's fool! I know how setups work – and you're setting me up!"

It was one of the rawest conversations we'd had up to that point. I knew about the corruption in Houston's law enforcement back then. His comments weren't surprising – they were consistent with what had come to light during investigations and scandals. His voice trembled, not with regret, but with a kind of pride and fear woven together. Like a man who thought he'd gotten away with something but now feared the price of being known.

When I pressed for details, he shut down. The window closed. But not before he left me with a cryptic remark.

"I took care of them, and they took care of me."

Another time, out of nowhere, he started asking questions about my mother – strange questions.

"Was your mother in a group home?"

"Was she blind and deaf?"

His voice wasn't casual. It was searching. He was trying to piece something together, trying to remember. It was like he couldn't recall which woman he had hurt, just that there were many. That moment was deeply unsettling. It was as if he was flipping through a mental catalog of past harm, looking for the one that matched me – looking for Sybil.

Yet, there were moments when I saw something that resembled humanity. Not often, and not reliably. But it showed up.

Doug had a small job helping elderly people run errands or get groceries. It wasn't much, just a few hours a week, but it gave him something to do – some sense of purpose. He talked about it more than you'd expect. I could tell it mattered to him. Maybe it was one of the few things he could point to and feel good about in his life.

By 2021, the pandemic had reshaped everything. Like many others, we started moving around more again. We made regular trips to Houston to check on Sybil and spend time with Joseph's children and grandchildren. Doug learned we were coming into town and asked us to visit.

We hadn't seen each other in person since 2012. For nearly a decade, the only connection had been occasional phone calls, which only resumed less than a year ago. Still, his voice had changed. There was less energy, less bite. He sounded worn down, and his breathing had grown labored. Eventually, I agreed to see him.

Joseph and I arranged a time and place. I wasn't sure what to expect, but the man who greeted us was not the one I remembered. Doug looked thin, frail, and slightly hunched. He moved slowly, relying on a walker and dragging along a portable oxygen tank.

He was no longer intimidating. He was vulnerable. It was strange seeing him that way.

We began seeing him more regularly during our trips. He took pride in showing us around his small corner of the city. He introduced us to neighbors and his property manager, and he even pointed out favorite spots around town. One of those places was Treebeards, a local restaurant he liked. A restaurant with fresh Southern-style dishes, where he occasionally enjoyed taking us.

He brought us to Christ Church Cathedral, where he attended early morning services. The space was beautiful, quiet, and reverent. We met his pastor. There was a kind of ceremony in those introductions. Doug seemed eager to be seen with us. There was pride in his voice when he called me his son. You could hear it. It mattered to him.

I noticed something then. For a man who spent so much of his life hiding, he was now reaching for something he'd never had – connection. Family. Recognition. Maybe even redemption, though that word felt too neat for what was happening.

He didn't have much. No wife. No other children. No legacy. But when he introduced me to people, I could tell it gave him something. A place. A role. A connection.

On one of those visits, he looked down, his voice barely above a whisper.

"I wish I had known about you sooner," he said. "It would've given me a reason to do better. Something to live for."

It was the closest thing to an apology I'd ever get.

Later, he took us to see Alice Luna – the woman who had been a kind of mother figure to him, and the person who had helped bridge the gap between us. Her home was unlike anything I expected. The walls were covered in paintings. Her work was everywhere – on the walls, on shelves, on easels tucked into corners. The colors, the brush strokes – it all told a story. She had talent, and her art brought life into every room.

She greeted us with warmth and genuine affection. When it was time to leave, she hugged us like family. It felt familiar. Safe. For a moment, it reminded me of what belonging can feel like – simple, unspoken, complete.

On another trip to Houston, Doug asked me to go to lunch with him – just the two of us. No Joseph. That was out of character. He had never made a point of excluding Joseph before. I tried not to read too much into it, but the request unsettled me. It was a four-hour drive from Garland to Houston, and for him to ask for time alone felt deliberate. Unusual.

What was the reason? Why now?

I was cautious but curious, so I agreed.

We met for lunch at a small, quiet place near his apartment. Doug seemed more anxious than usual. He didn't talk much at first. Just looked at me, then down at the table, then back at me again. When the server left us with our drinks, he reached into his coat pocket and slid an envelope across the table. Inside was $2,000 in cash.

"I want to donate this to help your mom," he said. "I heard she's been having a hard time."

I didn't know what to say. Sybil had recently become homeless. A few weeks prior, I had set up a GoFundMe to help her get back on her feet. Doug had somehow found out – maybe through Alice or someone else – and decided to contribute.

Given his limited income, it surprised me. He didn't have savings or assets. That money came from what little he had. Maybe it was guilt. Maybe it was an attempt to help, even if it didn't erase anything. I didn't analyze it too much. I just thanked him. It was the first time he had done something that genuinely benefited Sybil.

In February 2022, we packed up our lives once again. Joseph was offered a new role – Area Director in the Chicago Region, overseeing twenty-three Social Security offices in Metro Chicago and Northern Indiana. It was a huge step forward for him. For us, it meant another relocation.

We sold our home in Garland. Spent about two months in temporary housing. Then we bought a place in Miller Beach, a quiet little community tucked along Lake Michigan, in Gary, Indiana. Once again, I was on the job hunt. That constant cycle – packing, adjusting, starting over – had become strangely routine for us – controlled chaos.

Moving to Indiana cut off our in-person visits with Doug. From then on, our relationship existed only over the phone.

He called often. Some conversations were light. Some wandered. Others left me drained. He told stories that didn't always make sense, like his supposed romantic involvement with his housekeeper. The story changed depending on his mood. He was clearly lonely, and maybe the fiction helped him feel a little more alive.

I didn't argue. I didn't correct him. If that story gave him a sense of dignity, I let it stand.

Sometimes I needed space. The emotional weight of our conversations lingered. I didn't always have the energy to pick up his calls. When I didn't, his response was usually cold or quietly manipulative.

"I thought you weren't going to call back," he'd say.

Or worse, he'd answer with a detached tone, letting me know I'd disappointed him somehow. It became a pattern. If I didn't reach out within a few days, he'd act like I'd abandoned him completely. He wanted contact, but it had to be on his terms, in his time. That wasn't always possible for me.

Still, there were days when we talked like two ordinary people trying to connect across years of silence and damage. I asked questions. Small, harmless ones. Sometimes random. Sometimes deliberate.

"Who was your first girlfriend?" I asked one afternoon, just trying to lighten the mood.

He paused, as if sorting through dusty boxes in his memory.

"I don't remember," he finally said, "but I remember the first time I had sex."

He went on to tell me about visiting a prostitute at age 13. Arranged by a relative. That stuck with me. It didn't explain everything, but it revealed something. Something about how early experiences had twisted his understanding of women, of sex, of power.

Not everything was heavy, though.

In one of my more playful moments, I asked, "What's the stupidest thing you've ever done?"

He didn't even blink.

"Robbed the checkout guy at Kroger's – with a line of people behind me and no weapon," he said, then burst out laughing.

I didn't know what surprised me more – the absurdity of the story or the ease with which he told it.

It was ridiculous, but it was real. That kind of honesty – raw, unapologetic, unfiltered – showed up more and more in our talks. Not often, but enough to keep me engaged. Enough to remind me that he was, for all his flaws, human. Just a man sitting in the ruins of his life, trying to make sense of it all in the only way he knew how – through stories, whether true or not.

He didn't ask for forgiveness. He didn't offer explanations. But he stayed in contact. Sometimes that was enough. Sometimes it wasn't.

There were days I wanted to hang up the phone. Days I wished I hadn't picked up at all. And other days I found myself listening closely, wondering if he'd slip and reveal something important – something I hadn't heard yet. He rarely did.

But I kept listening.

He spoke often about his struggles with anger and the anger management programs he had completed. He asked me once if I ever struggled with anger myself. I gave him a vague answer. I didn't tell him everything, but I understood the question behind the question. Maybe he wondered if any of his traits had found a home in me. He wanted to know if the worst parts of himself had somehow traveled down the bloodline.

Over time, our conversations turned more personal. He kept me updated on his health with a surprising level of openness. It started with texts that included scan results, sometimes images from MRIs or PET scans. Then there were lab reports, discharge notes, and doctor summaries. It became routine. He never explicitly asked me to respond or interpret anything – he just sent them. I think he just wanted someone to know. To witness what he was going through.

Then came the documents. He named me as his next of kin. Designated me as his medical power of attorney. There was no dramatic conversation about it, no buildup. Just a message telling me it had been done. I didn't know what to say. It felt like something he didn't know how to ask for, but something he quietly needed.

He never asked for anything directly. Not once. Sometimes, he'd mention having trouble finding an item like a particular type of sock or a small health device. It was never framed as a request. But I picked up on it. I'd heard Alice describe the same pattern from her time helping him – coded comments, subtle cues. So I ordered the things he mentioned. Compression socks, a pulse oximeter, heating pads, and multivitamins. Amazon made it easy. He'd never say thank you in a grand way, but I could tell he noticed.

By early 2023, Doug's health took a sharp turn. After a biopsy, something shifted in his body. He said he didn't feel the same afterward. His voice on the phone had a dull edge to it. He described experiencing back pain that lingered and deepened each day. After a week of trying to push through, he was rushed to the emergency room.

Within hours, they moved him to the ICU.

The hospital staff began calling me regularly. They explained everything with clinical clarity, always careful with their tone. His condition was serious and declining daily. I tried to keep up – to understand the jargon, to follow the reports. At the same time, I kept talking to Doug. Each day, his voice was weaker, but he still wanted to talk.

Then, in the middle of all this, COVID hit us.

We had avoided it for three years. We were cautious – more than cautious – especially with Callie's medical fragility. But it didn't matter. On Monday, March 20, Joseph tested positive. We tried to isolate, clean, and disinfect. By Tuesday, I tested positive, too. Then, on Wednesday morning, Callie.

It hit hard. Not just physically, but logistically, emotionally, and practically. We couldn't move. Couldn't cook. Even standing up felt like a task. It was as if someone had drained us entirely of life and energy.

That same morning, Wednesday, March 22, 2023, I got the call from the hospital.

Doug was unresponsive. His organs were failing. They couldn't give me a definite timeline – maybe hours, maybe a day or two. They urged me to come if I wanted to see him.

I explained we were sick and stuck in Indiana. There was no way we could travel. It wasn't just impossible – it was unsafe for everyone involved.

I contacted Doug's church and asked them to send someone. I reached out to Alice, and she immediately went to the hospital. I was grateful, but it also made the distance feel even heavier.

A few hours later, the phone rang again.

I can't recall the exact words. Just the voice. Calm, maybe too calm. A nurse or a doctor, I can't be sure. What I do remember is the moment – me sitting on the couch, dazed, looking out the living room window. As the nurse spoke, a hearse pulled up outside our house.

For a second, I thought I was hallucinating. The timing was too surreal. I even said to the nurse, half-lucid and floating in a COVID fog, "I sure hope he's not trying to take me with him."

Eventually, I realized what was happening. Our neighbor across the street had passed away. She had been in hospice for a while. The hearse was for her, not for me. Still, the irony struck me sideways. The overlap of moments. The sound of death from two directions at once.

The days that followed blurred together. We were too sick to leave the house. Too sick to plan anything. No energy for grief or logistics. No energy for anything at all. We just lay there – recovering from the virus while carrying the weight of another loss.

Doug had no spouse. No partner. No children except for me. His family was physically distanced. I handled the hospital details. The cremation. All from afar while recovering from COVID.

Joseph and I talked briefly about holding a memorial. But nothing could happen while we were recovering. So we paused everything. No rushing. No formal decisions. Just space.

On Tuesday, May 23, 2023, we arranged a funeral service for Doug, but because of Callie's condition, Joseph stayed behind to care for her. I flew alone from Chicago to Houston.

The church was beautiful – arched ceilings, warm wood beams, and sunlight filtering through stained glass windows. It felt ceremonial, even sacred. But it was quiet. Small.

Carly, Joseph's daughter, came with me. Alice arrived with a few of her family members. The rest of the guests were from Doug's church community. There weren't many of us – fewer than twenty. With so few in attendance, we all sat together in the choir loft, close to the altar.

There was no hiding the scale of the room compared to the number of people, but the service didn't feel empty. It felt concentrated – more direct. The absence of a crowd didn't take away the significance. If anything, it added a kind of rawness to the moment.

Rev. Blake Ridge delivered the eulogy. He spoke with measured care. It was clear they had been friends. He didn't soften Doug's past or pretend it never happened. He named it – without hesitation. He acknowledged the boundaries the church had placed on Doug's involvement. Doug had only been permitted to attend the earliest Sunday services when no children were present. That restriction spoke volumes, but he didn't linger on it. He moved forward with a sense of grace, recounting Doug's presence in the church, the ways he tried to show up, the quiet discipline with which he approached the final stretch of his life.

I sat listening as Doug's only family member in the room.

His relatives in Alabama couldn't make the trip but joined via live stream. Joseph and Callie watched from Indiana. Everyone else was a stranger, loosely tied by shared moments in a sanctuary.

Doug had been cremated. His remains were laid to rest at Christ Church Cathedral. After the service, I spoke with Alice and a few of the congregants. Most had known only the last version of him – the one softened by time and sickness, more subdued than the man who had once shaped my entire existence through absence and violence.

After the service, I was given a copy of Doug's will. It was straightforward. I was listed as Doug's only surviving son and the sole beneficiary of his modest estate. There was no surprise – just finality. Doug had left me a small amount of cash, which helped with his final expenses. His possessions went to the church. His car went back to Alice.

There was no sentimental urge to hold onto his things. No boxes of memories. No family heirlooms. What Doug had left behind wasn't physical – it was structural. He'd rearranged my understanding of who I was, what it meant to be his son. And what it didn't.

In the days that followed, I thought about what our relationship had become.

It wasn't redemption. It wasn't reconciliation, but it was something.

We spoke as two men, one at the end of his life, the other halfway through it, trying to connect across decades of silence. There were no apologies deep enough to erase the impact of his actions. No conversations long enough to explain everything away. But we spoke anyway. About pain. About anger. About things we had carried alone for too long.

One of Joseph's cousins, Randy Hughes, has a saying I never forgot: "If you look hard enough, you can find a little bad in the best of us – and a little good in the worst of us."

Doug was proof of that. A man who did terrible things. A man who left behind damage that could never be undone. Yet, even in that mess, there were brief flashes of something else. Humanity, maybe. Regret. Awareness. I can't say for sure.

I never saw him as a victim. I never excused anything. But I didn't see him as only a predator, either. I saw him as someone who had committed harm – and then, at the end, tried to be known, in whatever limited way he could manage. I let him be known, in whatever limited way I could allow.

There's no symmetry to it. No neat resolution. Just pieces. Fragments of truth. Some of them are painful. Some, surprisingly ordinary.

Justice for Sybil never came. That door was shut long before I ever stepped through it. But I found something else – something difficult and unsatisfying and oddly necessary.

In speaking to Doug, I stepped into the shadow of the past – not to fix or rewrite it, but simply to face it.

Sometimes, that's the only way forward.

Chapter 11: Reasonable Doubts, Relentless Questions

Let me be clear: what follows in this chapter is theory. My theory.

Everything up to this point – names, dates, records, testimonies – has been built on fact. Verified, reviewed, and cross-checked. I've pored over medical files, examined court transcripts, studied autopsy reports, and traced testimonies. But now, we're stepping into where facts end and patterns begin. Where conclusions can't be proven beyond a reasonable doubt, but where logic, history, and context point toward something undeniable.

These theories – my theories are the result of years of study – painstaking research, quiet interviews, and long nights reviewing cold files and old leads. I've sat across from investigators, journalists, and people who spoke in half-sentences and nervous glances. The stories I've been told don't always come with receipts but from people who've seen too much to stay silent. And over time, the patterns started to surface.

To understand how I derived these conclusions, I need to take you back to the 1970s.

Houston was a city in transition – trying to grow and polish itself, while rotting at its foundation. It wasn't just rough around the edges. It was compromised from the inside out. No place reflected that decay more than the Houston Police Department.

This wasn't just about a handful of dirty cops. This was systemic. A department where misconduct wasn't the exception – it was the expectation. An environment so saturated with corruption that the public stopped being shocked. Abuse of power didn't require whispers. It made headlines.

Evidence vanished. Some destroyed, and some conveniently never logged. In other cases, it was planted. Criminals operated freely, protected by relationships forged behind closed doors. Courtrooms became battlegrounds for those seeking justice, where injustice prevailed. Innocent people were locked away to close cases quickly.

At the core – the center of it all – stood Police Chief, Carrol Lynn.

Lynn had been a rising star in Texas law enforcement, but his leadership didn't clean up the department. It made it more efficient at protecting itself. The badge wasn't a symbol of trust. It was leverage. People on the inside knew who to protect, who to silence, and who to frame. Official reports read like fiction. Internal investigations went nowhere. And the louder someone yelled for accountability, the faster they found themselves on the margins.

Meanwhile, Houston's homicide rate climbed. And yet, certain cases – certain families – never saw closure. Under Lynn's tenure, the department became a machine powered less by justice and more by intimidation, secrets, and unchecked authority. A deep scar on the Houston Police Department was created by allegations of internal cover-ups and rogue units operating like street gangs with badges.

Citizens, especially those in black and Latino neighborhoods, spoke of illegal surveillance, intimidation, and brutality with no recourse. Civil rights attorneys fought case after case in court, and still, the culture held. In a city where trust in law enforcement was already eroded, they had no meaningful path to justice. There was no appetite for reform. Just denial.

It wasn't just Houston that was experiencing such upheaval. Similar stories played out in other cities, but Houston was on a different scale and depth. The rot ran through every layer of administration, going from the highest-ranking detectives to the officers on patrol.

And Carrol Lynn? He didn't just allow it. He shaped it.

The name Carrol Lynn still lingers in Houston's history like a toxin in the bloodstream – never fully flushed out, never quite forgotten. For a short span of less than two years, Lynn wore the title of Police Chief. It was supposed to symbolize integrity, order, and leadership – the very foundation of the police department. But under his watch, the Houston Police Department lost all claim to those words. His reign turned the city's law enforcement into something unrecognizable – a festering network built on secrets, surveillance, and unchecked power. Lynn didn't just fail the public; he disfigured the very institution he was charged to lead.

Whistleblowers began to come forward – some in whispers, others louder – but the system was designed to silence them. Rogue units operated with impunity, patrolling the city like paramilitary squads with guns and badges. It was less about keeping peace and more about maintaining control.

Still, Lynn stood tall. Publicly calm. Always composed. He spoke in polished language in press conferences about public service and safety. But behind the curtain, he was a strategist who knew how to manipulate silence, loyalty, and fear to keep the machine running.

Until the machine broke.

In 1978, the rest of the country caught a glimpse of what Houston had been living with. ABC News aired an explosive documentary titled *Lawless Police*. It pulled no punches. What had long been whispered in neighborhoods, hinted at in columns, and buried in closed-door hearings was now broadcast into millions of homes. America watched in disbelief as the stories unfolded – stories that felt more like crime dramas than real life.

When the verdict came down – guilty – Houston didn't erupt in celebration. It exhaled. Not because anyone believed Lynn was innocent. No, most people already knew what he was. The surprise wasn't the conviction – it was that it happened at all. That someone like him, with that much power, could be held accountable. It shattered a dangerous belief: the system would always protect itself.

Lynn's sentencing wasn't just a personal downfall but a public reckoning. His conviction didn't fix the system, but it made clear that the rot had reached the top. And that meant no one could pretend otherwise.

It's important to say this plainly: not every officer in Houston was corrupt. Some men and women took their oaths seriously and fought for justice even when surrounded by dysfunction. Some tried hard to change things from within. Some paid the price for speaking up. Lynn's reign shouldn't define every badge, but it did define an era.

For Houston, it was a moment of reckoning. For the Houston Police Department, it was a stain – deep, wide, and indelible.

The machine had fallen – the system failed – but not without casualties.

It was the corrupt machine, the untouchable system, that swallowed men whole. It was in this environment that Doug, my father, was deeply embedded.

I remembered a conversation I had with Doug years ago – one of those moments stood out. The day he descended into a paranoid rant because he thought I was setting him up.

"I worked with law enforcement," he had told me. Not *in* it. Not *as* it. *With* it.

"Did a few things for the department back in the day," he said aggressively, "handled things they couldn't be seen doing."

Working – as in doing favors for the police. Dirty favors. And at that moment, things started to make sense – especially what happened on December 23, 1978.

That night, Doug forced his way into the home of Leroy "Buddy" Giese. He moved with purpose. He didn't demand anything at random – he demanded money. He knew what he was there for.

At first, the story felt like chaos involving a man losing control. But the deeper I looked, the more deliberate it became. The details were too specific to ignore.

Buddy had recently lost his wife, Martha. A month earlier. That alone should've left him grieving, possibly alone, but when Doug showed up, Buddy wasn't alone at all. He was with Learlene – his ex-wife. Learlene, who by then was married to another man entirely. What was she doing there? Why were they together? Why did Doug go to *that* house on *that* night?

It kept tugging at me. When I eventually followed that thread, it led me straight to Martha – Buddy's dead wife. She wasn't just another name in the obituaries. She had a record, a case, a whole history buried under official silence.

Martha was about to go on trial for murder.

That should've stopped me in my tracks, but it didn't. I wanted to know more. I pulled court documents, arrest records, and media clippings. What I found didn't clear anything up – it made things worse.

Martha had been charged in connection with the fatal shooting of Melvin Schott. But the details around it were murky. The whispers surrounding the case said she was taking the fall for someone else – Buddy – that he had pulled the trigger, not her.

Then came the car accident. November 1978. Just weeks before Doug broke into Buddy's house.

According to the official report, Martha was pulling out of a driveway onto Main Street in Houston when a vehicle struck her at high speed – no indication of who was at fault. No charges filed. No follow-up investigation. Just a statement, a name, and silence.

I spoke to various family members of the deceased – both Melvin and Martha. Each provided a different version of the story – and none corroborated the official police report or autopsy. One stated that Martha was involved in a high-speed chase. They claimed someone had been following her, that she was scared and panicked. That she wasn't just driving – she was fleeing something or someone. Another said the family had always been told the accident was a suicide – Martha was driving at a high rate of speed and chose to end her life by running into a concrete embankment.

I pulled the accident report again. Looked up the name of the officer who filed it. And that's when things took another turn.

That officer had a record, too – not just of service, but of questionable conduct.

In April 1975, he was investigated for the killing of a truck driver. The ruling? Justifiable homicide. He stayed on the force. Just a few years later, in 1979, he was charged again – another homicide. This time, after a grand jury investigation, he was discharged from custody on February 2, 1979. No conviction. However, shortly after that, he left the Houston Police Department altogether.

Why did this man's name show up on Martha's file?

Was it just a coincidence? Did his presence there mean something? And if Martha was under pressure – if someone thought she might flip and testify – it's not hard to imagine how her death could be... convenient.

I kept asking myself: *Was this an accident, or was it dressed up to look like one?*

I found no evidence of a formal investigation into her death. No second look. No press coverage beyond a short obituary. A woman set to stand trial for murder suddenly dies in a car crash, and no one digs deeper?

That doesn't happen by mistake.

Then there's the man who hit her. His name's on the report, but that's all. No charges. No arrest. No legal follow-up of any kind. It's like the collision didn't exist beyond that paper trail. No accountability. Just another dead woman in the margins of a city trying to clean up its image.

The closer I got to this, the more it became clear – Doug's attack on Buddy and Learlene wasn't random. It was calculated violence. Was it tied to something? To Martha? To whatever secrets she held, or whatever power Buddy thought he had after her death?

What happened on December 23rd wasn't the beginning of anything. It was a continuation. The system had been broken long before that night. Doug was simply playing his part – still doing those "favors" he once mentioned. The kind that doesn't show up in the official record. The kind that gets paid in silence.

So, when I look at that night now, I don't see a man who lost control. I see a man who knew exactly where to go, who to confront, and how to make it look like something else.

When Doug stormed into Buddy's house that December night and said, *"You owe me money,"* it sounded simple. But I've learned that with Doug, nothing is ever simple. That phrase – those four words – had layers. Was it about money? Or was it a message? A job? A clean-up?

Doug once told me, in that flat, unaffected tone, "I intimidate people who owe debts."

He didn't say *I used to.* He didn't say *for myself.* Just that it was something he did. A service.

Was Doug somehow involved in Martha's death? Could that be why Buddy owed him money?

All a coincidence?

The more I dug deeper, the more it didn't smell like a coincidence. Its stench suggested a cleanup.

So I looked backward.

October 1978.

Two months before Buddy and Learlene were attacked.

Three women. One murdered. One survived. One left for dead.

All three were sexually assaulted.

At the start of the month, on October 2nd, Gayle Ann Cater's body was found. Abducted, raped, murdered, and dumped in a canal. A 22-year-old woman was discarded like she didn't matter. At the end of the month, on October 30th, my mother, Sybil, was discovered. Abducted, raped, left for dead. Then, somewhere in the middle – sandwiched between the attacks on Gayle and Sybil – the unidentified woman. Abducted and raped, too, but she escaped.

Three female victims within a month. What were the similarities? How did the dots connect?

The location: Same area. East Houston. A one-mile radius.

The canal: Gayle's body was dumped in a canal in Chambers County. That much is clear. The same general location where the unidentified woman said she escaped. And then Buddy's own words in the police report came back to me – his account of what Doug said to him: "I could kill you and throw your body in the canal and get away with it."

That didn't sound like a bluff. It sounded like a reference.

Doug didn't say that as a threat. He said it like it was a fact. Like it was something he *knew*, as if it had worked before.

I went through every scrap of paper I could get my hands on. Incident reports. Victim statements. Court records. It all kept circling the same drain.

Three women.

The profile: young, vulnerable, beautiful women. All three pulled from the same neighborhood. None of them were high-profile. No media coverage is worth anything. Not then.

The description: The account from the unidentified survivor was short but precise: a man from Alabama with blue eyes, driving a truck. That detail hit hard. My DNA exists because my mother, Sybil, was assaulted by a blue-eyed man from Alabama who drove a truck. That's not theory. That's a fact. My existence is the *Walking Proof.*

October 1978: three attacks, all within weeks. Gayle Cater, the unidentified woman, and Sybil. December 1978: the attack on Buddy and Learlene Giese. Four events. Four victims. One dead, three survived. One child was born. The threads of these four crimes woven together created one unnerving narrative.

Direct Evidence: Medical records proved the assault on Sybil. DNA tests confirmed my paternity. I was the only living link between that October night and the man who attacked her. I didn't just have questions. I had biology.

Buddy and Learlene's case, on the other hand, was thoroughly documented. Police reports, court transcripts, and eyewitness statements were all accounted for. Doug was named, charged, and found guilty. The language in the reports matched what I already knew – forced entry, violent confrontation, demands for money, physical assault, and rape.

Doug, my father, was the confirmed perpetrator in both cases.

Circumstantial Evidence: On the surface, the events surrounding Gayle Cater and the unidentified victim might be written off as coincidental, yet with each new thread of evidence, the notion that this is mere chance becomes increasingly difficult – almost impossible – to accept.

I remembered Doug's words again – read in the report from the Buddy and Learlene case: "My attorney is Percy Foreman, and I will not give an interview without him." That line might sound like bluff or bravado to someone unfamiliar with the name. But Percy Foreman was no ordinary attorney. He had represented some of the most notorious defendants in American criminal history. For Doug to drop that name so casually, like it was normal, said a lot.

One attorney to represent Doug was Charles Melder. He handled headlines such as his involvement with the Elmer Wayne Henley serial killer case. Henley played a part in the Dean Arnold Corll case – also known as the Candy Man murders. A case that drew national media attention after the discovery of 29+ victims in Houston. All teenage boys – sexually assaulted – killed – and disposed of in mass graves.

Another attorney to represent Doug was Fred Heacock – a former Harris County District Attorney who'd later switch sides and become a high-powered defense attorney. Heacock knew the system from both sides of the aisle.

This raised the question: How could Doug – jobless, with a growing list of criminal charges – afford any of this?

He had no steady employment, no assets, and no trust fund. His only history was arrests, court appearances, and parole violations. Yet here he was, flanked by top-tier legal protection. That kind of representation wasn't random, and it wasn't cheap.

It reminded me of that call with Doug when he said, "I took care of them, and they took care of me."

Digging into the 1974 case – where Doug stood trial for the rape of a minor – I found court records that didn't line up with justice. While records verified that officers were called to testify, their actual testimonies were not available. The case went before a grand jury; however, it never went to a formal trial.

Doug found out I knew about this case. His explanation of how the charges were reduced from rape to "indecency with a child" was simple. Uniformed officers, law enforcement professionals, took the stand *for* Doug, not against him. They weren't called to provide facts or verify the sequence of events. They vouched for him.

What Doug said didn't make sense. Why would multiple officers put their names on the line to defend a man accused of sexually assaulting a child? Was the answer already in front of me? Doug had said it himself: "I took care of them, and they took care of me."

That wasn't paranoia. It was position. Access. Support.

Were the people who should've stopped him the same ones who covered for him?

We've now stepped out of the 1970s, a decade that closed with Doug being sent to prison from 1979 until 1985. When he reappeared in the mid-1980s, it was in the shadows of Galveston, Texas City, and La Marque, Texas. I suspect the power and protection he relied on in the 1970s had slipped away. Yet, the people who lingered around him – and the unsettling events that trailed him – suggested he had not changed.

Looking for anything that explained the connection, I found an address listed for Doug: 1030 Maple Street in La Marque, Texas. A plain house in a quiet neighborhood.

According to court documents, the home was owned by Kelly Templet.

This wasn't just where Doug lived. It was where several men with long rap sheets also lived – men with records for rape, assault, and drug trafficking. At different times, Doug's name appeared to be connected to several of his roommates.

Was this just a random house? Was it a hub? A revolving door for violent and sexual criminals?

I found no indication that it was registered as a halfway house. I was unable to locate any official license or public record suggesting it operated as anything other than a private residence. But something about the pattern stood out. Why did so many repeat offenders with similar crimes all end up tied to this one location?

Did Templet offer low-rent housing to criminals or knowingly run a place where people like Doug could come and go without questions? Either way, it was clear: 1030 Maple was more than just a mailing address.

Was the list of men who shared 1030 Maple Street with Doug random? Many names came with a record, and the charges weren't minor.

Richard Garner, for example, was charged with aggravated assault with a deadly weapon after he pointed a loaded gun at a woman's head. In the same incident, he was also charged with assault by choking – a violent, hands-on attack with clear intent to harm. Garner lived at 1030 Maple long enough to list it as his residence in official documents.

Another tenant, William David McMillan, didn't just have a record – he left a paper trail soaked in brutality. According to court records, William assaulted the very man who owned the house, Kelly Templet. The report said William beat Kelly so severely that he fractured three of his ribs and damaged a ligament. He used a knife and a gun to threaten him. The confrontation ended with William taping Kelly's wrists and ankles with duct tape before leaving him behind, injured and bound inside his own home. This wasn't a scuffle. It was an orchestrated attack, and it happened at 1030 Maple.

Then there was James Sidney Jernigan. His name showed up again and again, frequently tied to the same addresses as Doug – three times between the 1980s and 1990s. James wasn't just another roommate with a bad attitude. He was wanted in connection with the sexual assault of a seven-year-old girl. He had a long-standing criminal history, one that closely mirrored Doug's. The two of them didn't just pass each other in the hallways. They moved around together.

Three addresses. Three separate times. Different years, same pattern.

And this was just what could be verified through court documents and housing records. The public data didn't cover every move, but the overlap between Doug and men like Jernigan pointed to a pattern of association, not coincidence.

There were moments when I wondered if I was missing something. Maybe this was all a coincidence. But there was no other explanation for the kind of insulation Doug had around him – officers testifying on his behalf, high-powered lawyers in his corner, and a home base in a house full of other criminals. The network was quiet but well-formed. No headlines. No attention. Just a steady system of protection and silence.

That silence was what kept him moving. Through courtrooms. Through neighborhoods. Through victims.

I had reason to suspect that by the 1980s, Doug's crimes went further than officially recorded. The details aligned too closely with one of Texas's most disturbing unsolved cases – the cluster of disappearances and murders connected to a desolate stretch of land between Houston and Galveston.

They called it the Texas Killing Fields.

Roughly 25 acres of marshy, undeveloped land that became synonymous with death. From the 1970s through the 1990s, dozens of women and girls vanished near that corridor. Some were found, their remains scattered across the field. Others were never recovered at all. The press called it a dumping ground. These weren't crimes of passion. They were systematic. The killers knew the land. They knew the routes. And they knew how to disappear.

Doug had lived near there – close enough to drive by it daily, close enough to hide something without being noticed.

His timeline matched the killings. So did his behavior. By the time some of the earliest disappearances occurred, Doug already had multiple assaults on his record. His violence wasn't impulsive – it was controlled. Planned. And unprovoked.

He had access. He had transportation. He had a history of coercing women into vulnerable positions and threatening them into silence. That's exactly the kind of offender that fits the profile of the Texas Killing Fields suspects.

Some people I spoke with had a theory that mirrored my own. There was a network of offenders rather than a single killer. That network, they believed, included Clyde Hedrick.

Clyde's name showed up repeatedly in investigations tied to the Killing Fields. He was ultimately convicted of involuntary manslaughter in the death of Ellen Beason, a young woman whose body was found after Clyde initially denied even knowing her. Although he was questioned in connection with other cases in the area, no further charges stuck.

I spoke directly with two investigators familiar with the Killing Fields cases. They confirmed there had been a known connection between Doug and Clyde. When I pressed further, they didn't elaborate. One referred to it as "a smoking gun," but neither offered documentation nor specifics. It was a dead end. Still, they didn't deny it.

Doug's name was never publicly linked to the case. There were no formal charges, no official interviews that made it into the case files – at least none that were accessible. But the associations were there. His proximity. His network. His methods.

In October 1988, Suzanne Rene Richerson was working the night shift at Casa Del Mar Condominiums in Galveston. She was 22 years old. Sometime between 6:00 and 6:30 a.m., she disappeared without a trace. Witnesses reported nothing. There were no signs of struggle and no surveillance footage to analyze. She was there – then gone.

Suzanne became one of the 34 confirmed victims tied to the Texas Killing Fields. Her body was never found.

She matched the general profile of several other victims – young, working-class, alone at the time of the abduction. Her disappearance occurred during a window when Doug was not only free but actively living within driving distance of Galveston Island. He knew the area. He had lived in La Marque, not far from the Casa Del Mar complex.

No physical evidence ever tied Doug to Suzanne's disappearance. But again, the pattern held. Geography. Timing. Known behaviors. Known associates.

In 1989, a private investigator got a tip – anonymous, untraceable – that Suzanne Richerson's body was buried in the backyard of a house in La Marque, Texas. That residence was located less than half a mile from 1030 Maple Street, where Doug was living at the time.

The dig didn't last long. Forty-five minutes after it started, it was shut down. No remains were recovered. No warrant was issued after the tip, no follow-up search was conducted, and no public records of who placed the call exist. The lead came and went without consequence.

What stands out is the proximity. Doug could have walked to that property. He wouldn't have needed a car. He wouldn't have needed help. And yet, the location was never searched again.

The question that lingers isn't just who made the call – but why it was made. Was the tip legitimate, or a deliberate misdirection? It's impossible to know. However, when you consider Doug's behavioral patterns, the idea that he might have made the call himself isn't far-fetched. He had shown signs of manipulation before. He liked control. He liked watching the ripple effects of his actions. It's not hard to imagine him sitting back, just out of view, as investigators dug into the soil – knowing they wouldn't find anything.

Suzanne's remains were never located. Her case, like so many others linked to the Killing Fields, remains unsolved.

The more I examined the people in Doug's orbit, the more I questioned whether he operated alone. The violence was there. The intent was there. But the bigger picture didn't align with the idea of one man quietly orchestrating everything from the shadows. His movements seemed reactive, not strategic. He showed up where others were already in place. He followed rather than led.

Over time, through interviews, court records, and long conversations with my father, I believed that Doug wasn't the mastermind. He wasn't pulling the strings. He was taking instructions. He played a role – but not the central one. His violence was consistent with someone carrying out orders, not someone coordinating a larger operation.

What I found pointed to a more structured network. One that operated in silence, protected by the lack of oversight that came with jurisdictional gaps and bureaucratic failures. There were always connections – Doug to Clyde, Doug to James Jernigan, Doug to other known offenders. Some connections with direct involvement in the Texas Killing Fields murders. But those connections didn't start or end with him. They pointed outward, linking a chain of men who passed through towns like La Marque, Dickinson, and Galveston, each insulated by the others.

Some of them had records. Others stayed just clean enough to avoid official suspicion. But when you lined up the names and addresses, the overlaps became impossible to ignore.

My search, at times, felt like I was chasing ghosts. A name here. A detail there. Nothing conclusive, but it's always just close enough to keep me searching. I'd sit for hours following any thread that might lead to answers. And somehow, Doug always turned up. Like a warped version of Where's Waldo, his face or name would appear in places it shouldn't. A quiet witness. A friend of someone involved. A name just outside the margins.

It wasn't conclusive. But it was consistent.

Three cases, however, are documented without ambiguity. In 1974, Doug was charged with sexually assaulting an underage girl. He was sentenced. The record exists.

In October 1978, he raped Sybil. She survived. Her account is on file. DNA and paternity tests conclude I am the *Walking Proof.*

Two months later, in December 1978, Doug attacked Buddy and Learlene Giese in their own home. He sexually assaulted Learlene at gunpoint in front of Buddy. That case went to trial. The details were presented in open court.

These aren't rumors. These aren't guesses. They are verified cases, each backed by court transcripts and surviving witnesses. And yet, even these brutal acts failed to define the extent of his violence fully.

Doug's criminal record is measurable. His impact isn't.

There are names we'll never know. Stories that were never filed into reports. Were there women who didn't come forward? Children who couldn't? Did law enforcement in the 1970s have the tools or the framework to connect interstate offenders or cross-reference crimes committed in neighboring counties? What Doug did in Brazoria County wasn't necessarily linked to what he did in Galveston or Harris counties unless someone drew that line intentionally.

The gaps weren't always due to negligence. Sometimes, they resulted from a fragmented system. However, in Doug's case, the fragmentation worked in his favor. He moved without notice. He slipped between jurisdictions. He changed cities and roommates and never stayed in one place long enough to raise alarms.

Much of the information in this chapter is speculative. While grounded in research and intuition, it is not definitive proof.

In the end, everything you've just read rests on a fragile lattice of hunches, theories, and circumstantial evidence. There's no confession, no smoking gun – just fragments pieced together by intuition and shadowed logic. But sometimes, the truth hides not in what's proven but in what's suggested. Sometimes, you must read between the lines to connect the dots.

Chapter 12: Born of a Storm, Carried by the Tide

As I sit on the sand, toes sunk deep into the warm grains, staring out across Lake Michigan, the breeze moves gently through the tall grasses, stirring the dunes behind me. Waves rise and fall in a rhythm that is steady, almost meditative. Just beyond the shoreline, Chicago breathes. I can see it faintly – its towers softened by distance, the hum of the city silenced by the stretch of water between us. Out here, it feels like I've stepped away from all of it, not just from the noise, but from time itself.

This place – this quiet curve of shoreline – is a space where I can exhale. I came here to find clarity and get away from the pressure and emotions that have been tightening around me throughout the writing of this book. It was not just the content that was heavy – it was what the content required of me. This wasn't a writing project; it was an awakening.

Layer after layer, memory after memory, each chapter pulled something up from the deep. Things I wasn't sure I'd ever have the strength to face, let alone write down. What started as a search for answers about my mother's rapist became something more.

This book isn't only about what happened to her. It's about me. My existence, my identity, my fight to shape a life in spite of where I came from. And it's about truth – the kind that doesn't always come with clean lines or clear resolution. You have to dig for it, sometimes blindly, until it surfaces in bits and pieces. Enough to show you what's been hiding beneath.

Nothing about this process was clean. The research. The interviews. The long hours spent combing through court transcripts, newspaper archives, property records – documents that held pieces of a past I didn't live through but still carried. There were nights I barely slept, nights I couldn't stop myself from playing the same scenes over in my head – Doug's name on reports, my mother's story echoing in medical records, the dates, the names, the places.

It was hard to look away from the small, painful facts that proved what we already knew but were never supposed to say aloud. I'd been tracing ghosts. Some of them were mine; some of them were my mother's, but all of them were heavy.

Still, I kept going.

Not because I needed to prove anything to anyone, but because I knew this story deserved to be told. The silence surrounding it had lasted long enough. As hard as it's been to keep pushing forward, I never doubted that it was necessary. Not once.

But sitting there, I was struck by something else. Something I didn't expect to feel – not now, not like this.

Gratitude.

Not in a generalized, everything-happens-for-a-reason kind of way. That's not how I see the world. Gratitude, for me, is specific. It's the way my husband has stood beside me for sixteen years – never pushing, never pulling – just there, steady. Patient. Listening when I needed to unravel something aloud, holding space when I didn't have words. He didn't sign up for this part of the journey, but he didn't flinch when it came.

His family, too – my family now – welcomed me in long before they ever understood where I'd come from. They loved me as I was, without explanations or conditions. That kind of belonging was something I didn't grow up expecting. I used to believe I was too damaged to deserve it. Too strange. Too marked. But they never saw me that way. They saw someone worth loving. And their love became something I could trust.

There's power in that. In being seen without being dissected. In being valued without having to earn it. When you spend your early life unsure of where you stand, love like that feels almost unreal. But it's not. It's right here. It's real. And it's mine.

That doesn't erase the past. It doesn't fix the harm or change where I came from. But it gives me a place to stand while I face it. A solid ground beneath my feet as I look back, dig deep, and try to understand the shape of the truth.

For now, I sit here and breathe. The wind is cool, and the sand is still warm from the last rays of the setting sun. The lake keeps ebbing and flowing with the tide like it always does. Nothing has stopped. Life keeps going.

And so do I.

The facts I've laid bare in this book are part of my past – but they don't define my future. They sit behind me like old photographs: sharp, undeniable, but not the whole picture. Yes, the past was brutal. Yes, it left scars. But it also proved something I didn't know I was capable of – resilience.

Not the glossy, overused version people throw around to sound inspirational, but the kind that shows up in silence, in showing up again and again when no one is watching. I didn't just survive. I climbed. I built. And I've shaped something real out of the wreckage. Something beautiful created on top of something so broken.

I built a life that is steady. A life I chose. A life no one handed me.

My work in finance might seem far removed from all of this. Numbers. Markets. Strategy. It's not what people expect when they hear my story. But that's part of why it works. That world gave me structure. It gave me a place where outcomes weren't determined by emotion or chaos. It became a space where I could measure success by effort and logic, not legacy or blood. There's safety in that kind of order. There's comfort in building something that holds – even when everything else feels like it's unraveling.

I carved out a place for myself. I earned trust. I proved reliability. And in doing so, I created security – first for myself, then for others. That, in its own way, is resistance. A quiet rebellion against everything I was supposed to become. A refusal to be shaped by someone else's violence. I was never supposed to make it here. But I did. By choice. By action. Not by luck.

As the sunlight glistens off the surface of the water, I find myself thinking again about my genetic reality. It's not something I could avoid. My biological father was a violent man – a predator whose choices have left a ripple effect across lives, including mine. My mother, who brought me into the world, carried deep wounds of her own. Severe mental illness shaped much of her existence and, by extension, shaped mine. It's a complicated inheritance. Not the kind anyone hopes for.

There were times when I worried something in me would crack open, and I'd discover that I'd gotten the worst parts of them. Maybe the violence or the instability was written into my blood like a curse waiting to surface. Those questions came like crashing waves, sometimes without warning. I've had to face them. Not once, but many times.

The truth is, and I had to really sit with this to realize it: *I am not just biology.* None of us are. We are not a walking continuation of our biological parents' choices. We all make our own.

I've accepted that being born from something broken doesn't mean I'm destined to break. I've stood at the edge of my fears and decided to keep walking anyway. I've chosen therapy. I've chosen honesty. I've chosen love, even when it scared me.

That's what matters

The frightened child inside me – the one who still sometimes panics when the world feels unpredictable – has learned how to breathe through the questions. I've made peace with not having all the answers.

Faith has helped shape that understanding, though not in the way I once understood it.

The faith I grew up with was rigid and demanding. It came with rules, expectations, and shame. It left very little space for doubt or nuance. For a long time, I tried to fit myself into that mold. I tried to pray the right way, believe the right way, live the right way. The truth was, I was carrying too much weight, too many questions that didn't have answers that fit neatly into doctrine.

Over time, my faith changed. Or maybe I changed, and faith just followed. It's quieter now. Softer. It's not rooted in fear but in love, not in punishment, but in compassion. I no longer feel like I have to earn grace – it's just there, waiting.

This reformed belief has been what steadied me when the work of this book pulled me under. It's what held me when the truth felt too sharp to carry alone. There's room in this new faith for all of me. For the facts, the mess, the grief, the joy, the reality of what I came from, and the hope of who I've become.

The lake spread out before me, calm now. Its surface caught the light, then shifted with the breeze. It was always moving. Some days, it was still. On other days, it crashed. But it never stopped. Watching it reminded me of healing. Not a straight line. Not a checklist. But a series of waves – some gentle, some wild. But always in motion. Always changing.

I've learned something about truth along the way. Telling it doesn't erase what happened. It doesn't undo the hurt or make the past easier to accept. But it does shift something. It makes space. It breaks the silence that protected the lies. It lets light into places that were kept in the dark for too long.

That doesn't mean the pain disappears. It doesn't mean everything feels clean or resolved. But it does bring relief, even if only in small moments. A kind of freedom – not the dramatic kind that people write songs about, but the quiet kind that lives in your body. The kind you feel when you no longer have to pretend.

That's enough for me.

When I think of my biological father, I realize I didn't go looking for him. I didn't wake up one day curious to find out if the man who hurt my mother was still alive. I was just trying to understand myself and make sense of the gaps in my history. The story found me before I had the words to ask for it. But once I knew – once the DNA came back and there was no room left for doubt – everything shifted.

There's something unexplainable about standing across from a man who's responsible for your existence and your mother's trauma. The kind of moment you never prepare for, because how could you? I walked into that space not knowing what I'd feel – anger, grief, fear – but I didn't expect the calmness that would wash over me.

I didn't expect to feel so steady. But I was. When he denied everything with a straight face, I didn't raise my voice. I just let the truth settle between us. It didn't need to be loud or powerful. Sometimes, the quiet is more damning.

He spoke his lies easily, the words slipping out smoothly like he'd said them a thousand times before.

"I never hurt a woman."

In a calm, steady voice, I held him accountable. I let him feel the weight of his own lie in the presence of someone who exists solely because of what he did. That was the justice I had – maybe not the kind a courtroom would give, but what life and fate dish out.

That moment gave me something I didn't know I needed. Not closure – I don't believe in that – but clarity. There was no longer a shadowy figure in my mind. No more guessing or wondering. He was real. He was there, and he couldn't outrun what he had done.

It also gave me an opening to look at my birth mother differently. All those years, I had questions I didn't know how to ask. I didn't understand why she made the choices she did. But facing him allowed me to see her in a new way.

Her silence made sense. She wasn't weak – she was surviving in the only way she knew how.

That understanding softened me. It made space for compassion toward her that I hadn't had before. Not out of pity but respect. I respected her for the way she was able to do something that could have broken her and still found ways to move forward. She didn't have to do it perfectly. She just had to make it through. And she did.

Forgiveness isn't something I talk about easily. It's not clean or simple or even always possible, but I had to reckon with it in ways I hadn't expected. Not because he deserved it. He didn't. But because I didn't want to carry the weight of his actions any longer. I'm not sure I forgave him fully. Maybe I never will. But I saw him as a broken, dangerous man, and for a second, that was enough.

What matters more is what I chose to do with that truth. I could've buried it, let it sit in the dark corners of my memory, and tried to forget. But I didn't. I put it on paper, gave it shape, gave it context, and by doing so, I gave myself something in return – freedom.

Writing this book wasn't an act of vengeance or revenge. It was reclamation. A way of saying: *This is what happened, and I'm still here.*

I refuse to pretend it didn't. There's power in truth, even when it hurts, especially when it hurts.

I don't know if this story will ever find its way into a police file or reopen a cold case. That was never the point.

I'm not a detective or a prosecutor. I'm just trying to make peace with the truth I never asked to carry and trying to understand the people who shaped my life without letting their choices become my own.

And maybe – just maybe – these pages will stir something more. A clue. A memory. A shift in perspective that reignites a forgotten investigation.

I still have questions that I don't have the answers to. Maybe I never will. But what I've learned is that even unanswered questions have value. They push us. They keep us honest. They remind us that what we don't know still matters.

This journey has pulled things out of me I didn't know I was holding. Some of it has been painful. Some of it has been healing. But all of it has been real. And in a world where so much is hidden or manipulated or forgotten, that reality matters.

And as I sit here, waves kissing the shore and the sky wide open above me, I feel something I haven't felt in a long time.

Peace.

With the sand slipping through my fingers and the wind blowing at my back, I realize that while this story may have begun in darkness, it ends in light. Not because the pain disappeared, but because I chose not to let it be the whole story.

I'm writing this chapter – my final thoughts now, in real time, as the lake breathes beside me. And with each word, I let go.

I know now that I was meant to tell this story. Maybe not for him. Maybe not even for her. But for me and for anyone else who's ever wondered if the truth is worth the trouble, it is. Every single time.

Whatever happens next – whether my story reaches one soul or many – I know this much:

I've told the truth.

And that is enough.

Chapter 13: Sources and Resources

Each narrative in this book represents a persistent quest for truth – an endeavor that required unconventional methods and significant effort to unveil. Piecing together this tangled web required persistence, creativity, and, frankly, a willingness to knock on some doors (both literal and figurative) that many people never would.

My research was a blend of the old and the new: dusty paper trails and digital DNA. Public records and private interviews. Police reports and family secrets. It wasn't just about gathering facts – it was about interpreting silence, decoding gaps in stories, and respecting the lives that once filled those blanks.

Much of this work would not have been possible without the cooperation and transparency of several agencies and departments. I want to extend my deepest thanks to the Harris, Chambers, and Brazoria County law enforcement agencies, along with the City of Houston, Pasadena, and Freeport, Texas. Your willingness to honor public record requests gave me access to case files, autopsies, court proceedings, and decades-old police reports. These were not just documents; they were voices from the past, waiting to be heard.

On the genetic front, the truth would've remained buried without the powerful tools offered by FamilyTreeDNA, AncestryDNA, 23andMe, and GEDmatch. Each platform played a unique role, and without their technologies, I would still be searching in the dark. DNA testing changed everything – offering not only clarity but the ability to trace the untraceable and connect families long separated by circumstance or secrecy.

This journey also brought me into contact with incredibly generous and trusting individuals who were willing to share painful memories in the service of the truth. I want to especially acknowledge MeeMaw Kennedy, the mother of Gayle Cater, who graciously opened her heart to me and allowed me into some of the most personal corners of her life. Your trust meant everything.

To Jenifer Atkins, the niece of Martha Grant Giese – thank you for helping me fill in the missing pieces of a complicated puzzle. Your insight was instrumental in giving voice to a woman who didn't always have one in her lifetime.

I also want to recognize the Evergreen, Alabama Public Library, and especially Sherry Johnston, for your warmth and resourcefulness. You didn't just help me pull records – you welcomed me like family and made me feel like this work mattered.

To all the branches and limbs of the Williams family, I appreciate each one of you who contributed, questioned, and pieced together your side of the story with me. And to Gordon Johnson, in particular – your extensive work on the Williams family tree provided a backbone for so much of this research. Your generosity and deep knowledge helped connect dots I didn't even know existed.

I didn't do this alone. Every page in this book exists because someone picked up the phone, opened a file, shared a memory, or simply let me sit and listen. Some of you handed over records. Others handed over trust. Both mattered. I can't overstate how much your time, your honesty, and your openness meant to me. Research can be a lonely thing, but this wasn't. At every turn, someone showed up to help carry the weight. Thank you for that – truly.

Please don't consider this a simple list of thank-yous. It's a reminder that stories like this are rarely uncovered alone. They require a community, a network of curiosity and compassion, and a willingness to believe that the past still deserves a voice. Thank you to everyone who helped me listen.

Made in the USA
Coppell, TX
10 January 2026

68108596R00131